Beat Your
Addiction

Hodder Arnold

A MEMBER OF THE HODDER HEA

Beat Your
Addiction

Trevor Barnes
Edited by Denise Robertson

Ventures

Hodder Arnold

A MEMBER OF THE HODDER HEADLINE GROUP

Orders: Please contact Bookpoint Ltd, 130 Milton Park, Abingdon, Oxon OX14 4SB. Telephone: +44 (0) 1235 827720. Fax: +44 (0) 1235 400454. Lines are open 09.00 to 5.00, Monday to Saturday, with a 24-hour message answering service. You can also order through our website www.hoddereducation.co.uk.

British Library Cataloguing in Publication Data
A catalogue record for this title is available from the British Library.

ISBN-13: 978 0 340 94318 2

First published   2007
Impression number 10 9 8 7 6 5 4 3 2 1
Year   2012 2011 2010 2009 2008 2007

Typeset by Transet Limited, Coventry, England.
Printed in Great Britain for Hodder Education, a division of Hodder Headline, an Hachette Livre UK Company, 338 Euston Road, London, NW1 3BH, by Cox & Wyman Ltd, Reading, Berkshire.

Hodder Headline's policy is to use papers that are natural, renewable and recyclable products and made from wood grown in sustainable forests. The logging and manufacturing processes are expected to conform to the environmental regulations of the country of origin.

ABOUT THE AUTHORS

Trevor Barnes is an award-winning journalist and reporter with BBC Radio's Religion and Ethics departments. He is the author of ten books including *Dealing with Depression*, a self-help guide to depression written with the endorsement of the Samaritans. He lives in London.

Denise Robertson's television career began with *BBC Breakfast Time* in 1984. She has been the resident agony aunt of ITV's *This Morning* for the last 20 years. In that time she has received over 200,000 letters covering a wide range of problems from viewers and from readers of her newspaper and magazine columns. She has written 19 novels and several works of non-fiction. Her autobiography, *Agony: Don't Get Me Started*, was published in paperback by Little Books in July 2007. She is associated with many charities, among them Relate, The Bubble Foundation, Careline and the National Council for the Divorced and Separated.

WHICH PAGE?

How can I spot the signs of addiction?
Turn to pages 4, 7, 12

I care for someone with an addiction; where can I find help? *Turn to pages 29*

How do I stop feeling so guilty about my problem? *Turn to page 70*

I feel so isolated? What can I do? *Turn to page 82*

What is detox? *Turn to page 108*

What is rehab? *Turn to page 113*

My children are suffering from my addiction. What can I do? *Turn to page 137, Chapter 6*

I feel I'm going to relapse. What do I do? *Turn to page 195, Chapter 9*

Has anyone else faced the problem I have? *Turn to page 243*

CONTENTS

FOREWORD

By Fern Britton and Phillip Schofield

As presenters of ITV's *This Morning*, over many years we have met many incredible people with many incredible stories to tell. What we have learnt is that life can be wonderful but it can also be very hard.

Our phone-ins have generated thousands of calls a day from viewers all over Great Britain looking for suitable advice on a range of subjects. What is very obvious from these calls is that we are not alone with the personal challenges we often face and there is a great need for help in dealing with them. We are always cheered by the follow-up letters and emails from viewers saying how our experts' advice has helped them to turn their lives around.

Over the 20 years *This Morning* has been on air, Denise Robertson, our agony aunt, has regularly offered support and advice to millions of viewers on a huge range of personal problems, and she spends even more time off-screen answering letters, calling those in distress and dealing with questions via the internet. As a result, she is uniquely qualified to edit these books which reflect the common sense and sensitive advice that we provide on the show.

We believe these survival guides will help you to deal with the practical and emotional fall-out caused by issues such as bereavement, relationship break-ups, debt, infertility, addiction, domestic violence and depression.

If you feel that your particular problems are insurmountable – don't! There is always a way to improve your life or at least get yourself on a path towards a new start. If you think you are alone with your problem – don't! Our experience shows that many of us face the same problems but are often reluctant to admit it. You have already made a great start by picking up this book.

We both wish you all the strength and support you need to tackle your own personal problems and sincerely hope that we can help through these books and through our continued work on the programme.

INTRODUCTION

I see addiction as an invader, something that takes over your life. In time, you become a non-person, a slave who must obey the invader's commands. That's no way to live, is it? Another reason why we need to conquer addiction is that all too often, someone turns to drink or drugs or gambling in order to escape a life that has become unbearably painful. Family arguments, broken relationships, trouble at work – there are a thousand things that can cause suffering. For a little while, the sufferer can escape that pain. A strong drink will anaesthetize a wound. Drugs numb pain and give a lift. If a horse romps home or three bells come up in a row, the world will be bathed in a rosy glow. Whatever your chosen remedy, it can bring temporary relief. Who can blame someone, therefore, for seeking out that relief again and again? Yet the painful effect of that release is that it robs you of the energy or the will to do something about the cause of the pain. Instead of improving your life, it renders you incapable of changing anything, and now you have a new burden – the cost, in both money and emotion, of supporting your addiction. It will rob you of family and friends, employment, leisure, money, and even the roof over your head. Over the years, thousands of people, young and old, rich and poor, have written to tell me of the hell their lives have become because addiction crept up on them. The letter often begins 'I can't believe this has happened to me'. Too often it ends 'I know there's no way out'. And don't imagine that those people were in some way flawed or born to be 'victims'. Addiction can happen to anyone. The good news is that anyone can, with help, cast out the invader and reclaim their life. That's the purpose of this book, to point the way to freedom. Use its simple step-by-step approach and start your journey back to happiness. And please believe the book comes with the goodwill of everyone at *This Morning*.

Denise Robertson

ARE YOU AN ADDICT?

In this book we deal mainly with three of the most common types of addiction: alcohol, drug and gambling addiction. You could add to that list many more: addiction to sex or pornography, addiction to shopping or exercise, addiction to work or food, even addiction to the housework. You will find that much of the advice contained in the following pages applies equally well to other addictions.

What all addictions have in common is that they provide a pleasurable but all too brief sensation of well-being that feels preferable to the sometimes uncomfortable realities of life. In short, they offer an apparent escape from real life into an artificial world where all, for a time, seems well. The problem arises when the effects of your 'drug of choice' wear off and you are repeatedly craving a higher dose for a diminishing return. All the while, your behaviour is cutting you off from the real world – with a catastrophic impact on your health, personality, relationships and finances.

Problems often start gradually, beginning with harmless use that escalates into something uncontrollable. Nowhere is this more apparent than with alcohol. What could be nicer than a glass of chilled Chardonnay at a barbecue, more civilized than a good red with a meal, or more refreshing than a cold beer after a hard day's work? Social drinking is not only pleasurable, it is accepted and indeed encouraged. The question is: at what point does social drinking change into something more destructive and compulsive?

Try the following tests for yourself or use them on people you fear may have a problem. Tick any boxes that apply.

Spotting the signs of alcohol addiction

❏ Have you ever felt guilty about your drinking habits?
❏ Have you ever been worried by the amount you have consumed or the frequency with which you consume it?
❏ Do you often get drunk?
❏ Has drink ever affected your work?
❏ Do you often drink alone?

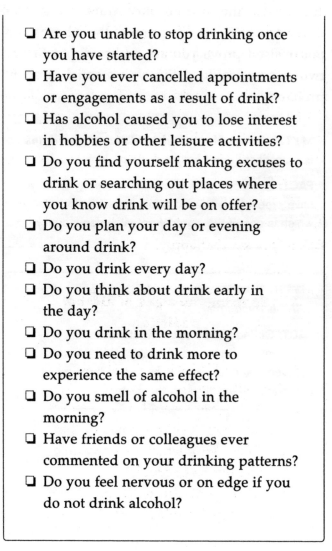

❏ Are you unable to stop drinking once you have started?

❏ Have you ever cancelled appointments or engagements as a result of drink?

❏ Has alcohol caused you to lose interest in hobbies or other leisure activities?

❏ Do you find yourself making excuses to drink or searching out places where you know drink will be on offer?

❏ Do you plan your day or evening around drink?

❏ Do you drink every day?

❏ Do you think about drink early in the day?

❏ Do you drink in the morning?

❏ Do you need to drink more to experience the same effect?

❏ Do you smell of alcohol in the morning?

❏ Have friends or colleagues ever commented on your drinking patterns?

❏ Do you feel nervous or on edge if you do not drink alcohol?

These are the classic indicators of alcohol dependency. Ticking any one of these boxes may not in itself prove you are addicted, but ticking two or more could indicate a potential or actual problem.

MYTH: Being able to drink a lot and not feel drunk is proof that I don't have a drink problem.

FACT: If you can drink a lot without feeling drunk you have probably developed a tolerance for alcohol, which is one of the signs of potential dependency.

MYTH: Taking a shower or drinking black coffee will sober you up.

FACT: Coffee has no effect whatsoever. The only thing that will rid the body of alcohol is time. It's believed that it takes between two to three hours for one drink to pass through the system.

Spotting the signs of gambling addiction

❏ Are you gambling more than you can afford to lose?

❏ Do you feel guilty about your gambling?

❏ Do you borrow money to finance your gambling?

❏ Have you gambled money you should have used to pay bills?

❏ Have you ever gambled in order to pay a bill?

❏ Have you gambled significant amounts of your or your partner's wage on pay day?

❏ Have you used savings to gamble?

❏ Has your gambling ever caused arguments or tension at home?

❏ Have friends and work colleagues noticed your gambling patterns?

❏ Have you spent longer than you had planned gambling?

❏ Have you ever 'lost your shirt'?

❏ Does your gambling keep you awake at night?

❏ Is gambling interfering in your relationships with partners and friends?
❏ Is gambling elbowing out other hobbies or leisure pursuits?

Ticking any one of these boxes indicates that it is more than likely you have a problem with gambling.

Q. What is problem gambling?

A. Problem gambling is a pattern of behaviour centred on the compulsive need and desire to bet. It involves spending more and more money more and more frequently on gambling – with negative consequences on relationships and finances.

Q. Is problem gambling just a financial problem?

A. No, it's a deeply rooted psychological and emotional problem with financial consequences.

Abusing prescription drugs

Prescription drugs are legal and associated with cure and getting well – because of this there is a common misconception that taking them is safe. This is true only under the appropriate conditions. The key word here is 'appropriate' – when doctors prescribe or recommend a drug, they do so knowing that it is appropriate for the patient's complaint or condition.

A bereavement, for example, can trigger medical conditions like insomnia or depression for which antidepressants, benzodiazepines or other sleeping pills may be appropriate. When the depression passes and your sleeping patterns have normalized, however, using sleeping pills may become inappropriate, and continuing to use them may be a sign of an unhealthy dependency. Taking a larger dose than has been prescribed or increasing the frequency with which you take the drug in order to prolong its effects is also inappropriate. Using prescribed drugs when they have not been prescribed – or lying to ensure that they are prescribed – is highly dangerous and damaging both to physical health and mental well-being.

> *MYTH: Abusing prescription drugs is safer than abusing illegal drugs.*
>
> **FACT:** Taking prescribed or over-the-counter drugs for a medical condition you do not have is very dangerous. It is just as damaging and potentially lethal as abusing illegal drugs.

We should also add that occasionally doctors themselves may be inadvertently complicit in a person's addiction because it is not obvious for how long a patient has been on a 'repeat prescription'. There are well-documented cases of people being on benzodiazepines (originally prescribed to them, for example, for sleep problems) for several years – with the result that over time they find it very difficult to come off them. Only a carefully controlled and medically supervised programme of withdrawal will allow a person to come off some drugs painlessly.

> *Q. Can drug addiction be treated?*
>
> **A.** Yes, given a professionally supervised programme of detoxification and withdrawal and the personal desire of the recovering addict to quit.

From the clinical perspective, antidepressants are not addictive although they can cause problems if stopped suddenly. For further information and guidance see the supplementary section on prescription drugs in Part 5. For the moment, however, if you are able to tick any of the boxes on the next page, it is likely you have a problem with prescription drug abuse. You should see your doctor immediately and be *absolutely honest* about the drugs you are taking. Lies, half-truths or evasions will make it impossible for him or her to diagnose your condition and draw up a gradual withdrawal plan.

Q. What is detox?

A. Detoxification is the controlled withdrawal of a substance or substances from the body.

Spotting the signs of prescription drug addiction

❏ Have you ever used a prescription drug when it has not been prescribed for you?

❏ Have you ever misled your doctor into prescribing a drug for you?

❏ Do you regularly use a drug when you wake up or go to bed?

❏ Have you ever used a drug without properly understanding or bothering to understand what it was intended for?

❏ Are you terrified of being without a particular drug?

❏ Is your drug use interfering with relationships and home life?

❏ Is your drug use preventing you from enjoying the simple pleasures in life – going for walks, meeting friends, enjoying the company of your children or grandchildren and such like?

❏ Are you prey to unexplained fears or panic attacks?

❏ Do you feel guilty or ashamed about your drug use?

❏ Have you taken a particular drug in ways not recommended by the manufacturers – for example, crushing pills and diluting them in water or dismantling slow-release capsules and ingesting the contents directly?

❏ Have you ever used anyone else's drugs?

Drugs, substance abuse, and the young: A quick guide for parents

Times have changed since the strongest drug with which people were likely to come into contact was an Aspirin! The range of stimulants, depressants, intoxicants, analgesics, mood-, mind-, and behaviour-altering substances is truly breathtaking, and the ease with which many can be obtained terrifying. The young are vulnerable to snares and temptations unknown until comparatively recently, and they deserve our support and help rather than just the unsympathetic, mindless condemnation so often expressed in the popular media.

It's beyond the scope of this book to explain why people (young or old) take drugs. Millions of words have been written about the psychological, emotional and sometimes physical pressures that make people seek temporary relief in drugs. Adding a few hundred more would make little difference. However, the one common reason – and it's an uncomfortable truth that parents, teachers, police and even governments choose sometimes to ignore – is that it feels good. People wouldn't inject themselves with chemicals if it didn't. And whether you're a high earning city worker snorting cocaine through a rolled bank note or a teenager sniffing glue from a crisp packet in the park, the same principle holds true: drug-taking is usually pleasurable.

If drug-taking doesn't always make you feel great, it certainly makes you feel better than you did; but only for a short time and at a terrible cost. If it didn't make you feel better, no one would become addicted in the first place. And if it *just* made you ill, nervy, depressed, nauseous, hopeless, lethargic, anxious, weak, and fearful, drug-taking would lose its appeal overnight. The fact is that it delivers an intense and pleasurable high that for a short time puts everyday life in the shade.

If you have abusive or neglectful parents, if you're bullied or pressured at school, if you have no one to open your eyes to the possibilities beyond your terrible high-rise flat, if you've got little prospect of a job and are bored or idle, or if you're lonely or isolated or simply out of tune with the pressures and shallowness of society as you see it, then drugs might appear to offer a 'solution' to your situation. We are not condoning drug-taking, merely confronting the reality that often lies behind the phenomenon.

Drugs are no respecters of social class or income, and the children of middle-class, affluent parents are just as likely to fall prey to the dangers of drugs as those from less fortunate backgrounds. Being brought up in a large house in the country, sent to an expensive boarding school or a top grammar school and having every convenience, gadget and privilege is no guarantee that your own child will not be a victim of this growing menace.

For some, drug-taking can be a passing phase; for others it can be a destructive addiction. If, for whatever reason, you're concerned that your son or daughter or grandchild is addicted to drugs, hold on to this reassuring thought – treatment works. It may take time and effort, struggle and tears but addiction can be broken. However, before it can be tackled, it needs to be recognized.

One misconception that can make recognition of the problem difficult is that young people become addicted only to illegal or street drugs. Wrong. There are lots of drugs openly and legally on sale over the counter that can become addictive. You may have some of them in your bathroom cabinet, or in the shed, or even in your shoe cleaning box. Solvents and glues, aerosols and nail varnish, shoe polish and cough mixture can all be abused in the search for that seductive high.

In fact, many youngsters think that 'legal' means 'safe' and that taking cough medicine, say, or combining it with alcohol and other things is an acceptable alternative to buying heroin or cannabis on the streets. While it's true that 'illegal' can mean 'dangerous' many perfectly legal and everyday substances are dangerous too. So how do you spot whether someone you know could be an addict?

> *MYTH: Cannabis is legal in the UK now.*
>
> **FACT:** Cannabis is still a controlled drug and is still illegal in the UK. Using and dealing are still arrestable offences.

> *MYTH: Cannabis is a soft and therefore safe drug.*
>
> **FACT:** Even moderate use of cannabis, especially in the young, has been associated with impaired concentration and behavioural problems. More significant cannabis use in the young also increases the chances of developing serious mental illness such as schizophrenia.

Possible tell-tale signs of addiction

- The appearance of being drunk without the smell of alcohol or the appearance of being high without the smell of cannabis.
- The smell of fruity cough mixture on the breath or the smell of pear drops or glue on the clothes.
- Red or wide eyes and dilated pupils.
- Empty bottles of cough mixture or empty blister packs of tablets stashed away in wardrobes or clothes.
- Sweating.
- Lack of vitality and interest in the everyday things of life.
- Irritability and sudden mood swings.
- Inability to concentrate.
- Lack of interest in school, college or work.
- Slurred speech.
- Scratching.
- Sudden attacks of panic or nervousness.
- Nausea and vomiting.

You may have suspected the worst and (courageously) confronted a young person close to you only to be met with the words, 'It's all right. I can handle it.' What do you say? It is probably best to say nothing for now other than to offer words of affection, support and sympathy. Then try persuading the person to take the following test and, in the privacy of his or her own space, to answer the questions honestly and in confidence, ticking any boxes which apply to them.

❏ Are you a regular or frequent user of illegal drugs?

❏ Have you ever stolen money or possessions to pay for drugs?

❏ Have you ever been frightened by the kinds of people you meet supplying drugs?

❏ Has drug use affected your performance at school, university or work?

❏ Has drug use interfered with personal relationships?

❏ Has your sex drive tailed off?

❏ Have you ever lied about how many drugs you use or about the frequency with which you use a particular drug?

❏ Have you ever tried to stop taking drugs?

❏ Has drug use interfered with your appetite or disrupted your sleep patterns?

❏ Are you terrified by the thought of running out of drugs?

❏ Do you, broadly speaking, feel unhappy?

❏ Have you ever experienced irrational fears or panic attacks?

❏ Have you used drugs to ease emotional pain or stress?

❏ Is your drug use disrupting your home life?

❏ Do all or most of your friends take drugs?

The more questions they answer yes to, the deeper the problem with drug abuse is likely to be. It is highly unlikely that they can 'handle it' and more probable that they have an addiction that is controlling them. We suggest seeking advice and help in the first instance from a doctor or from the list of charitable organizations at the end of this book.

Addiction can be reversed if the drug user is committed to a lifestyle change. We can not say that change will be quick or easy, but the positive message is that **change is possible**. Treatment works.

Part 1: What to Do Right Now

Congratulations! You've made the decision to confront your addiction (or someone else's) head on. That takes courage and strength, but it can also feel very disorientating. It's true that hundreds of thousands of people have been here before, but for you the experience is completely new and it's hardly surprising that it all feels very strange. So what next?

Moving forward

First of all, try to use this guide as a personal handbook. It won't offer any magical solutions but it will provide a clear, down-to-earth guide to the kinds of things you're going through at the moment. You don't have to read it in one go; you can dip into it when you need to. Take from it the advice that best suits your situation or modify this advice to suit your own circumstances and, above all, use it to convince yourself that you are not some kind of freak. **Many, many people are in exactly the same boat as you are right now.**

Next, take heart from the old saying, 'The journey of a thousand miles begins with a single step.' Over the next few pages, we'll suggest step-by-step strategies to get you through the jumble of emotional and practical problems facing you in the first days of your life changing decision. And then, like countless people before you, you may feel better prepared to make that longer journey, one step at a time, from darkness into light, from powerlessness into control, and from sickness into well-being.

It's quite likely, for example, that you'll be prey to huge mood swings: one minute feeling strong enough to take on the world, the next minute so frightened that you'd rather hide away from it; or yesterday you felt strong enough to kick your habit for good but today you are so weak and vulnerable that going back to your old ways seems to be the only bearable option. No wonder these times are compared to riding an emotional roller-coaster – forever up and down, never on the level. That's why we suggest that at first you take small, simple steps forward. Don't worry too much about the road behind you and don't get fearful of the road up ahead. For now, it's enough simply to be moving in the right direction. And you are, or you wouldn't be bothering to read this.

A word of warning

We are not a substitute for professional help and we don't pretend to be. We strongly suggest you seek out that help from a doctor, a fully qualified counsellor or therapist, or one of the many voluntary organizations with decades of experience dealing with the issues you face. Our hope is to complement what they can provide, to reinforce what they suggest, and gently to suggest and encourage. In short, we want to support you not only in the first few traumatic days, but in the months and years ahead.

A word for carers

Perhaps you are not an alcoholic yourself but you are married to someone who is. Possibly it's your son or daughter who's addicted to cannabis, cocaine or heroin and you desperately want to help them break the cycle of addiction. Perhaps it's your wife or partner who is repeatedly abusing prescription drugs without admitting it. Or maybe you're at the end of your tether with worry about a partner who's gambling away all the household budget. If so, we have advice on how best to seek help for those you love and care for – and also how to deal with the children of a recovering addict.

Either way, acknowledging there is a problem is the first step towards a solution. You have taken this first step and that's why, amid all the turmoil and the trauma, congratulations are in order.

Having recognized the problem, what do you do about it? First, resist the temptation to panic, go to pieces, or bury your head in your hands in despair. Recognition is a huge first step. And, once again, well done on getting this far. Now your problem has a name – addiction. Knowing the name and nature of your adversary makes you better equipped to deal with it.

Learn to talk honestly about the situation to other members of the household. Start by calling a family conference to discuss the problem and to set out your strategies for dealing with it. This doesn't have to be a high-powered conference with an agenda, note-taking and minutes read out by the chairperson, but there should be an air of formality about it rather than just a general chat in front of the television.

You could say something like, 'I want us to have a serious talk about X's illness. He needs our help and we need to talk about how best we're going to support him/her. So after tea, (suggest a convient time) I want us all to sit down together and talk about it.'

That way, you make it clear that this is a problem that's out of the ordinary and needs treating with a sense of seriousness and urgency. Switch off the television and radio, turn off the computers and video games, make a pot of tea and, without any distraction, talk. No books you will read (not even this one) can deal with your situation exactly because all people are different. Talking things through seriously as a family will enable you all to respond to the uniqueness of your own circumstances in a way tailormade to suit them.

If you've come this far, sweeping things under the carpet is no longer an option. Frank, honest and respectful communication – healing at the best of times – is particularly important now.

Think, too, about asking for support and reassurance from people going through the same thing as you. Al-Anon, Alcoholics Anonymous, Gamblers Anonymous and similar organizations (see Part 6) will be able to put you in touch with people like yourselves who are struggling to deal with the same problems. Knowing you are not alone can give you tremendous encouragement on both good and bad days. You might even find yourself getting involved at a voluntary level with such organizations and helping others.

1

Dealing with the immediate crisis

Let's not mince our words here. This is a crisis. Alcohol, drugs or gambling have brought you (and your loved ones) to a critical point in life, forcing you to make perhaps the biggest and most far-reaching decisions you have ever had to contemplate. However, there'll also be promise and hope, and opportunities you could never have dreamed of while the bottle, pills, or cards had you in their grip. Remember that the first step is the hardest, and you've just taken it.

Go easy on yourself. Don't beat yourself up for the things you've done; save your energy for something productive like doing things differently. That's where this book can help.

Are you in denial?

Let's start by being honest. No one's suggesting you're a liar as such but you've probably been in denial for some time. Denying you had a drink or drug problem or, if admitting it, insisting it was essentially under control. You may have told yourself a million times that you only ever had 'a bit of a flutter' because you were unable to admit that gambling was swallowing up your earnings (and more). You may have said you weren't an alcoholic but a 'heavy drinker' – while repeatedly stashing away bottles in the shed, in a filing cabinet or in a drawer at work. So be honest with yourself. Try one of the tests in the introduction and admit the scale of your drinking or drug use. It may surprise you.

MYTH: Binge drinking at the weekend and abstaining throughout the week doesn't qualify as alcoholism.

FACT: Possibly not, but by regularly drinking to excess (students may fall into this as a lifestyle choice), you are building up levels of alcohol tolerance that could be problematical in the long term. Blitzing your body this way can have adverse effects on your health; when completely drunk you also run the risk of having accidents, being mugged and even being raped.

Facing the problem

Knowledge

Facing the problem honestly means that you begin to know the problem for what it really is. If alcohol has been the issue, write down exactly how much you have been drinking in a typical week. Draw up a timetable of your drinking, at what time you had your first drink, how the day's drinking progressed, and at what time you finally crashed out. Add up the hours you were sober, merry, blind drunk or hung over, and add up how much you spent on drink that week.

MYTH: I can't have a prescription drug problem if my doctor is legally prescribing tablets and pills to me.

FACT: The combination of repeat prescriptions and the fact that most people don't always see the same doctor for every appointment means that it can sometimes be easy to continue obtaining repeat prescriptions without the doctor knowing how long you have been prescribed a medication for, and therefore not reviewing your continuing need. In addition, it may not be obvious to the doctor that you are collecting repeat prescriptions more frequently than you should be.

This information, recorded in black and white and in the cold light of day, may come as quite a shock. However, shocked though you'll might be, don't feel guilty or ashamed. As you see in a moment, such feelings belong to the category of negative and unproductive emotions, and if ever there was a time to be positive, this is it. Take a good hard look before filing the information somewhere safe; it will come in useful later.

Q. What is a safe level of drinking?

A. Department of Health guidelines in the UK suggest a maximum of 21 units of alcohol per week for a man and 14 units for a woman. A unit is roughly defined as a half pint of beer, a single pub measure of spirits, or a small glass of wine (125 ml). It's also recommended that you have two or three days a week when you drink no alcohol at all.

MYTH: I can hold down a job so I can't be an alcoholic no matter what I consume.

FACT: Many alcoholics are in very high powered jobs that make many demands on them. It is their constant preoccupation with alcohol that defines them as an alcoholic, not their ability to function between bouts of drunkenness.

Communication

Next, be honest with your partner. He or she will probably have known the truth for longer than you think, but hearing it from you will be an immense relief and prove that you're really serious about changing your lifestyle. If you've been a chronic gambler, for example, you can both look honestly at the household finances and best decide how you're going to pay off your debts and build up savings. If you don't have a partner, find an ally. Citizens' Advice Bureaux, community centres, addiction organizations, banks and church groups have free professional help and advice to enable you to manage your income and take control of your affairs once again.

MYTH: The UK government is once promoted 'Supercasinos' so gambling must be harmless.

FACT: It may be harmless for those who can afford to lose. It is potentially catastrophic for those who can't. Even those with the money to lose can develop a dangerous compulsion it is extremely hard to break.

Feelings

Once you've admitted the extent of your addiction, the chances are that you'll feel a mixture of emotions: shame, guilt, fear, loneliness or even anger. To start, try to manage the negative emotions of guilt and shame. Don't feel ashamed – as you'll see in a moment, it isn't helpful. Concentrate only on the things that will get you better, not on those that will drag you down.

Addiction is a massive and widespread problem for which you'll need a helping hand, a listening ear and, more often than not, a sympathetic shoulder to cry on. Being addicted and seeking help for your addiction **are not signs of weakness**. Admitting you need help is a sign of inner strength. You will find, to your surprise, that there are many men and women out there who are only too ready to help if you ask.

MYTH: A spell in 'rehab' will sort everything out.

FACT: The process of recovery will not be complete in a matter of weeks, even months. The detox process followed by rehab is the first step in a process lasting years. Long-term wellbeing requires a commitment to be sober or clean for the rest of your life. There are no short-cuts.

Seeking medical support

If your addiction has immediate medical implications, be honest with your doctor. That way the doctor can, in return, be honest with you about the clinical harm you've been doing to yourself and about what you will need to do to reverse it. Admit exactly the amounts of alcohol you have consumed and still consume. You'll probably be tempted to play them down. So get that timetable out and read it aloud word for word – down to every last half pint while waiting for the bus and every last miniature to get you through the afternoon.

If you've been abusing prescription drugs, you must be absolutely frank with the doctor about what you have been taking, how often, and in what quantities. Coming off such things as benzodiazepines, sleeping pills or anti-depressants is not a matter of just stopping. Sometimes the dose may have to be carefully regulated and reduced over time by a medical professional in order to minimize the withdrawal symptoms and the harm. The cliché really is true: honesty is the best policy.

Now to practicalities.

2

First things first: Practical

Carers

If you're not the addicted person but your partner is (or you fear he or she may be heading that way), it's as well to be prepared for the moment they confront the reality of their addiction. Some of what follows is worst-case scenario stuff and frankly pretty scary. Yet for some the reality of addiction will sadly only hit when the worst happens – overdose, alcohol poisoning or collapse. Let's hope you don't end up here, but the truth is that a small proportion of people will.

Prepare for medical emergencies

If things have come to a head and there is a potential medical or life-threatening emergency in your home, you need to know where you can get help. In the UK the 999 emergency services will obviously be on hand but it's as well to know the location of your nearest Accident and Emergency hospital unit. Keep the number of your local surgery to hand as well as any out of hours numbers. Update them regularly and keep them in an easy to find spot by the phone. Have the number of a sympathetic friend or neighbour listed too, in case you need emergency child care to cover your absence while taking a family member to hospital.

If your loved one is showing all the signs of acute drug/alcohol dependency (or withdrawal) then they should not:

- Drive
- Cook
- Smoke in bed
- Handle hot liquids
- Supervise children.

If you think the drug or alcohol use is increasing, be on the lookout for the following danger signs in your partner or friend:

- Vomiting or acute nausea
- Shaking or sweating
- Hallucinations
- Fits
- Disorientation and forgetfulness
- Blackouts
- Foam at the mouth.

Make sure you're ready to get immediate medical help if such symptoms emerge.

If a collapse or drug overdose happens (involving many of the above symptoms), phone for an ambulance immediately, stay with the person and pass on all details to the attending paramedic.

This is the most serious stage of addictive behaviour – when real danger to life and limb is possible and when specialist medical intervention is called for. Being ready for any of these things will help to prevent you from feeling shocked and powerless if they do happen. Having an action plan and relevant phone numbers to hand will stop any delays in seeking appropriate treatment.

'Recreational' drug users may also experience collapse and overdose – often in clubs where visibility is at a minimum and noise at a maximum. Learn to see warning signs in others, for example:

- Dizziness
- Nausea
- Headaches
- Sudden cramp or tiredness
- Shortness of breath.

If, while on the dance floor your friend experiences any of these symptoms, take them away from the dancing and the noise to a quieter spot, and allow their body to relax and cool down, slowly offering small amounts of mineral or tap water.

If your friend shows signs of panic or disorientation, take him or her to a quieter location and try to calm them down. If symptoms continue or get worse call an ambulance.

In the case of things like:

- Hyperventilation
- Narrowing of the pupils
- Erratic breathing
- Semi- or unconsciousness
- Blue-ish pallor to the lips and skin,

you or your friend may be in danger of collapse, coma and death. **Seek medical help straight away.**

Addicts

Get professional help

Your doctor is the first port of call. He or she will give you a thorough examination and be frank about your medical condition – both now and in the future. Your doctor may give you an ultimatum – carry on drinking like this and your liver will pack up in six months' time – or – keep on drinking as you are and you're heading for a heart attack. This may not make for comfortable listening but, one way or another, these are the facts you will have to incorporate into your new life. If you don't know already, your doctor will tell you that excessive alcohol consumption can lead to:

- Liver failure

- Heart disease

- Strokes

- Diabetes

- Muscle wastage

- Cancer of the mouth and oesophagus

- Psychiatric problems.

Your doctor can suggest a course of treatment, a detoxification programme or a rehabilitation centre that will be appropriate and within your means.

Next, contact a specialist organization geared to the needs of recovering alcoholics. The best known, of course, is Alcoholics Anonymous whose step-by-step programme has brought hope to millions (see page 328). Here you will receive a warm and non-judgemental welcome from people who, often from first-hand experience, know exactly what you are going through and who can give you the kind of support and understanding you need at this vulnerable time in your life.

Q. Can alcoholism be treated?

A. Alcoholism cannot be cured but it can be successfully treated given a determination on the part of the recovering alcoholic to give up drinking and to follow a tried and tested recovery programme. Recovering alcoholics can go on to lead healthy and happy lives.

Take responsibility for your health

Eating well

Your addictive lifestyle will have undermined a lot of your energy and immune system so you need to build up your strength again with a healthy diet. Healthy does not necessarily mean organic or expensive or any current food fad you may have seen in the paper. It means simple food, simply cooked – the sort of food you can buy at any market, greengrocer, supermarket or food store in the country.

Try to eat three regular meals a day, getting off to a good start with porridge or cereal, wholemeal toast and a banana, say, or yoghurt and cereal in the mornings. Avoid fatty fried breakfasts and eat simply cooked meals including foods high in protein, vitamins and carbohydrates. Cut out fast food and ready meals if you can and try to eat lots of fresh fruit. Include in your new diet things like:

- Fish and poultry
- Pasta and rice
- Dairy products such as cheese and eggs
- Fresh vegetables and fruit.

Adapting to a new diet of healthy food simply prepared may come as a shock if you are used to eating things like crisps, chips and burgers as fuel before your next drink or your next fix. Good food was probably not a priority; you had no time for it. Now you have, so re-educate your body to appreciate it. The taste of healthy food may take a while to get used to, but persevere and you'll appreciate the difference. Also any treats you allow yourself will be all the more delicious. Try to drink plenty of water during the day, and if you're a heavy tea and coffee drinker go for the decaffeinated versions.

Living well

Get into a healthy lifestyle with regular exercise. This doesn't mean you have to join a gym and buy all the fancy lycra gear. Walk into town instead of taking the bus, walk upstairs instead of taking the lift or go for a stroll in the early evening instead of flopping down in front of the telly. If you've got out of the habit, start to do the washing and cleaning!

Get a good night's sleep. Try to get regular early nights and rediscover the sheer joy of waking up early in the morning with a clear head. Avoid sleeping during the day so that you can get into a regular sleep pattern.

Sort out your finances

If gambling has been a problem, your finances are probably in a mess. Sort out your debts now – seek advice on managing and rescheduling them. Make all the economies and savings you can, and ask for time to meet your financial responsibilities. If your gambling has left you with serious tax problems, phone the Inland Revenue. It's actually not the impersonal machine you may have thought it to be – experienced advisers will view your case sympathetically and work out a schedule of repayments. The same with utilities; gas, water and electricity bills list a phone number to dial if you're experiencing problems paying. Phone the supplier and get the reassurance they can offer.

Make a detailed statement of incomings and outgoings and a note of all outstanding debts. If you or your loved one has had alcohol problems, they will also have been eating away at the family budget. Or perhaps you or they have lost a job altogether. Money problems can add to the pressure you're already under so sort them out as an urgent priority.

Think about a rehabilitation or detoxification programme

After talking to your doctor and a suitable support group like Alcoholics Anonymous (or similar), decide if you can actually be treated better at a residential rehabilitation or detox (drying out) centre. Alternatively, can your treatment be realistically provided and managed at home or as an out-patient? Choosing how you are treated has, of course, financial implications, and you'll need to think seriously about these.

MYTH: Gambling addiction is not a chemical dependence like alcoholism or drug abuse so, if you want to stop, it is just a matter of saying no.

FACT: Gambling may not have a chemical component, but its psychological pull is just as real and damaging as drink is to an alcoholic. In fact, particular 'chemical messengers' in your brain are released during the 'pleasurable' phase of addiction (for example, winning a large amount of money when gambling), making it more likely that you will want to repeat your addictive behaviour.

Avoid temptation

Remove all the temptations from the home. With alcohol, pour it down the sink if you must, or give it away to those who are better able to handle it. Remember, the problem isn't the drink; the problem is you, the drinker. Check out the range and variety of herbal teas. Buy lots of decaffeinated teas and some exotic juices. If you can stretch to it, buy a juicer to make your own healthy mixes. It's amazing what you can do with sparkling waters, crushed ice, tonic, sprigs of mint and slices of lemon. Buy a book on non-alcoholic alternatives to fill the craving of the 'cocktail hour' or the after-work pint. Sobriety need not be boring.

Have goals

You didn't notice it at the time, but your addiction was absorbing all of your time. In other words, now you've made the decision to give it up, you're going to have a lot of time to fill. And that's scary. However, remember that in every crisis there is danger *and* opportunity. So the free time is also fantastically liberating. Think of all the mornings, afternoons and evenings you've spent with drink or pills in your hand, unable to concentrate on anything else. It was as if they were the only things that mattered to you in the world. They *were* the only things that mattered to you in the world. They completely overshadowed your free time, your family and your friends, closing the door to all life's infinite possibilities. Now you have the chance to enjoy what life has to offer.

Why not learn a new skill, take up a new hobby or develop a new interest? Of course, no one's suggesting you immediately take up flower arranging or put a ship in a bottle, or learn rock guitar (although realistically nothing's stopping you any more), but you can spend your new free time doing all the sorts of little things you've been meaning to do if you'd had the opportunity. This might mean getting out in the garden or tidying up the shed or rearranging your CD collection. Having a goal – any goal, however trivial – will help you get through those difficult blank times that drink, drugs or gambling once used to fill.

Try to keep busy with any number of tiny, apparently mundane occupations – sorting out cupboards, clearing out your sewing box, shining shoes, looking for bargains on the internet – anything – and develop a routine that keeps you occupied. With your mind directed on other activities you'll be less likely to let it stray back to the old temptations. Make to-do lists, plan trips and try to transform every aspect of your life into a tangible goal – a mini-adventure where even the most ordinary task becomes an exciting and achievable challenge. You may find that the world so dulled by a haze of pills and alcohol is now full of real possibilities. You could experience natural highs that are far more pleasurable than the old ones – if only because they are more substantial and longer lasting. Sure, you may also experience the occasional low, but if you have an activity to take your mind off that pain and discomfort, you'll have a surprisingly effective weapon in your armoury of self-preservation. And that's where those lists come into their own. If you're feeling low, get out your to-do list and go through your tasks one by one. You'll find that every tick makes you feel just that little bit better about yourself. And cumulatively they'll add up to a greater sense of real and durable well-being. Go on, give it a try!

Put off all major decisions

You are under a lot of stress right now and this is not the time for the grand gesture. However tempting it might be to make a major decision that you hope will solve your problems in one stroke, our advice is simple: don't. Moving house, emigrating, having a baby or leaving your job are all fine things in themselves, but is now really the time to deal with the upheaval they'd all involve? One step at a time, remember. Sort out the problem of drug, gambling or alcohol abuse first then, when you've cleared the decks, you can consider other options. After all, one life change at a time is enough for most of us, isn't it?

Remember, too, that it's the small practical changes rather than the theatrical 'grand plan' that are going to be the most useful – and the hardest to pull off. You might say to yourself, 'We'll emigrate to Australia and start a new life where we can put the alcohol behind us.' But will it really work out that way if you haven't tackled the underlying alcohol problem already? Or will you just take the addiction to another part of the world and carry on exactly as you have been doing?

Bear in mind that a series of small, steady changes in your general direction and personal behaviour will most effectively get you to where you want to be. Compared to that, kitting out your future nursery, buying a place in the country or emigrating are easy!

Children

If you have children in the house, they'll be affected in ways that no one but they can tell. Even they may not have the words to make sense of the turmoil and the unease they're feeling. From a very early stage in the addiction, children may sense something's wrong at home but are unable to put their finger on it and this will make their fears all the worse.

There may be violent arguments, for example, shouting and screaming as one partner has a go at the other for his or her repeated drunkenness. Yet the deathly silences may be just as bad as mum and dad's refusal to confront a problem that's staring everyone in the face. While children are terrified by constant rows and raised voices, they're just as troubled by millions of perplexing and unanswered questions: Why is Dad always in bed until midday? Why does Mum's breath always smell so horrible when she puts us to bed? Why do I have to ask for supper when my friends have it put on the table at regular meal times? Why does my brother never leave his room? Why does my sister always seem to be in another world?

Children may also feel that all this mess is somehow their fault, that they haven't been good enough or well behaved enough to prevent this unhappiness being dumped on the family. Irrational and misguided, of course, but for them it's all too real and they will be blame themselves for what's happening to their parents, sisters or brothers.

Reassurance

Gently reassure your children that Mum or Dad or their big sister has a problem and that it has nothing whatsoever to do with them. Tell them it's rather like an illness (which it is) and that everyone's doing their best to cure it. Above all keep every channel of communication open, reassuring with hugs and soft words. If you're not the most touchy-feely of families, encourage your children to talk things over with someone they trust, an older brother perhaps, or an understanding auntie or friend of the family.

Children of alcoholics can become very withdrawn, lost in the confusion of someone else's unexplained moods and behaviours. They can seem blank and unresponsive and are reluctant to get excited about school trips, birthdays or treats. They know from bitter experience that the promise of a treat is usually accompanied by disappointment when one or other of the parents fails to deliver and the treat somehow never materializes.

At the other extreme, children can become very organized and overly mature as they adapt to a parenting role they have had to assume in the absence of a properly functioning parent. They suddenly find themselves having to prepare their own food, do their own shopping, cook for a parent who is incapable and look after their smaller brothers and sisters. In short, at an extremely young age they find themselves becoming the parent in everything but name. Heroic as this may seem, it can lead to problems in later life because they may never learn to be cared for themselves. As adults they may have great difficulty accepting help from others and functioning as part of a mutually dependent society. If you're in that position (or if you know someone who is), check the list of organizations at the end of this book for details of who to contact.

Being open

If you already care for someone with an addiction, it's easy to overlook the children. You've already got a lot on your plate and plenty to cope with. However, they're the vulnerable innocents in this drama, and often all they need is:

- Acknowledgement that there *is* a problem and it's not just in their imagination

- Reassurance that the problem is not their fault

- Reassurance that the problem is being dealt with.

It is also worthwhile letting the class teacher at school know that there are domestic tensions that may be affecting your child's performance and behaviour. You don't have to go into unnecessary detail and reveal everything about your partner's condition. Just make it clear that there are difficulties. A good teacher will probably have spotted the signs already and can make allowances for troubled behaviour.

3

First things first:
Emotional

You're beginning to make the first tentative steps towards recovery. You've recognized the problem, committed yourself (and others) to solving it, you're eating well, and you have established a working routine that's gradually freeing you of your addiction to drink, drugs or gambling. First of all, well done. Countless men and women over the years have told us how difficult even those 'simple' things are, and they are an achievement in themselves.

Guilt, shame and fear

You have things at the back of your mind – niggling things that are not as cut and dried and quantifiable as a healthy diet or a good night's sleep. These are complicated things that you don't seem to have the words for but which are eating away at you all the same. We can try and put them into words for you on the basis of tried and tested experience with people just like yourself.

You might feel that you've let people down, especially yourself, that you've let your parents down or that you're providing a poor example to your children. You may feel that you're a total failure who's made a complete mess of life and is now at the bottom of the heap while everyone around you is happy and successful.

Perhaps you feel guilty about the effects your behaviour has had on your relationship with your husband or wife, your children and your friends. You might feel guilty about the damaging effects it's had on your family fortunes, about the damage it's done to your prospects at work, or about the outrageous and embarrassing things you've done while drunk or drugged. Can you ever look your children's teachers in the eye again, for example, let alone their friends' parents at speech days, sports days and parents' evenings?

You might feel a paralysing sense of shame at the depths to which you sank, at the misery and pain your loved ones experienced as a result of your past behaviour. You may even feel a complete and utter disgust at the things you once did while in the grip of an addiction. Just thinking about these things sends a shudder down your spine and, what's more, you can't get them out of your mind. It's as if the video of your past life just can't be erased and is programmed to play back endlessly in your head. It's a real torment that constantly taunts and threatens to undermine your good intentions.

Then again you may be frightened that you'll never really beat this thing. Perhaps you're terrified of being swallowed up and consumed by it – so much so that you don't think you'll have the strength ever to overcome it. And because you don't think anybody other than you can really understand the agony you're going through, you probably – and understandably – feel pretty lonely.

This is a potent mixture of emotions to be dealing with. No wonder your life seems inexplicably and incomprehensibly chaotic just now. Moreover, just when you thought guilt, shame, failure, fear, and loneliness were enough to be dealing with at the present moment, what about a bit of anger to throw into the mix?

Anger at yourself, at your weakness, at your parents, even at the world for dumping this whole mess on your shoulders, or at your colleagues and friends who can apparently manage to gamble and drink heavily without getting themselves into the state you have. This is tough, but every day you survive without a drink, a bet, or a hit will make you stronger and your journey a little easier. In the pages following there is advice on how to manage your emotions. Try to take heart from it; it has helped many before you.

Learning to manage guilt

Addiction is a complex illness with all sorts of emotional and psychological extras that you don't find, for example, in arthritis, eczema, or glaucoma. But it's an illness all the same.

You don't feel guilty when you catch a cold, do you? Do you feel guilty when you break your leg, get a migraine, or come down with a bout of shingles? No. You shouldn't feel guilty for being ill, and yet perhaps you do. So how can you manage this feeling? At this point, we're going to introduce a bit of jargon. It's our hope that this guide is approachable, user-friendly, and jargon-free but we're introducing this particular bit of jargon because it's so useful. In the sections that follow you'll come across it so often that it's as well to get it out of the way once and for all. The term is 'cognitive therapy'. Essentially it is a talking cure that appeals to your head when you're feeling ruled by your heart.

Your feelings may be a cauldron of chaos and confusion distracting you from the task in hand: getting better. The cognitive approach tries to go beyond that confusion with a direct appeal to your rational mind. For instance, you may *feel* that you've achieved nothing and that your cravings are just as strong as they were. There's no hope; you're just going to go back to your old ways. Cognitive therapy (which really just means 'forget your feelings for a moment and just look at the facts') says, hang on a minute, you *have* actually achieved quite a bit. You've come clean about your problem, you've sought help *and* you haven't had a bet or a drink for a fortnight. This is a real achievement whatever misleading non-rational information your feelings may feed you.

Applying the cognitive approach to an addiction can be helpful in so far as it rationalizes what has become a real illness and tells you that there is no point feeling guilty about a condition over which (until you actively sought help) you had no control. It tells you effectively that it's pointless to wallow in negative guilt when what you really need to do is think and act positively.

However, having said this, it is worth pointing out that a little guilt is not necessarily a bad thing. The realization that your gambling, drug use, or your drinking has had a damaging effect on those close to you – and the remorse you feel for having hurt them – can be a powerful inducement to change. It can push you into thinking that you must never again harm your loved ones (and yourself) in that way. In small doses, guilt pulls you up with a start. It makes you face up to the wrong you have done and decide, from now on, to change your behaviour for the better.

Ultimately, people are responsible for their own actions. Whatever we do has consequences for ourselves and for others, and we have to own up to the wrong and the good we do. It may sound harsh, but at one level excessive drinking, regular gambling or illicit drug use started out as an action made consciously and in free will. And at one level, you have to accept that it's partly your fault that all this happened; if only because it's no one else's. There may have been extenuating circumstances (divorce, sadness, rejection, bereavement, depression, unemployment, peer pressure, temptation), but no one except you took the decision to drink the vodka, swallow the pills or buy the scratchcards. Remember that non-alcoholics have been bereaved and divorced too! But – and it's a big but – once the compulsion took over and developed into a full blown addiction you were then driven by forces largely outside your control and any talk of fault and blame becomes meaningless. The addiction then became an illness and you can't be blamed for being ill.

Consequently, while a little guilt may be useful when thinking about and acknowledging the damage you've done to yourself and your family, excessive guilt is not. A little guilt can be the spur you need to make amends in the future (and healthy proof of personal responsibility for your actions), but excessive guilt will leave you in an unhealthy state of paralysis unable to make the changes you need.

As we'll repeat so often in this book: **set yourself some goals**. Transform the negative feeling into a positive action, and start with a list that might read like this:

From guilt to action

- I've let my children down. I'll start taking them out more or I'll spend time playing with them.

- I've let my husband/wife down. We'll start doing things as a couple again.

- I've squandered our money. I'll make economies – or let my partner take control of the finances.

- I've neglected my friends. I'll phone them up more and visit.

- I've neglected my health. I'll eat and exercise sensibly.

- I've wasted my time. I'll spend my time productively on a hobby, or on tidying the garden, or on learning a new skill.

You may have done some pretty dreadful things in an excess of drink, drugs and gambling, but wallowing in a sea (or more likely a cold bath) of guilt is unproductive. If, however, that guilt is a spur to action then it's part of the process of healing. *Doing* something is always better than *worrying* about it. You'll be surprised how, once you've decided to change, people who you thought would remain disgusted by your past behaviour will be ready to forgive and forget, and accept the new you.

Q. Can you be a problem gambler even if you don't bet every day?

A. Frequency is not necessarily the determining factor in problem gambling. This is measured more by the emotionally and financially destructive consequences of the individual's pattern of gambling.

Learning to manage shame

Shame is an emotion altogether different from guilt and potentially far more corrosive. If guilt gives you sleepless nights over what you've done, shame tortures you for being who you are. To say you've done bad things in the past implies you can do better things in the future. To simply say you're a bad person means you can never hope to change, and that simply is not true. Everyone can change; you or your loved one has already started that process of change and, maybe in only a small way, has changed already. You need to remember that. But shame will not let you do so. 'I'm worthless.' 'I'm inadequate.' 'I'm no good.' 'I'm not good enough.' 'I'm unlovable.' 'I'm a bad person, a weak person, a useless person.' These are the kinds of feelings shame provokes. It can make you want to run away and hide from friends you believe think you unworthy of friendship in the first place. This sense of shame can cut you off from those around you – causing you to withdraw from the very people who might be best able to help.

If ever there was a time for the cognitive approach, (see page 71) this is it. To be able to move on, you need to be persuaded and ultimately

MYTH: *Admitting to being an addict is shaming and demeaning.*

FACT: Addiction is a disease not a vice over which you can exercise control. If anyone is going to disapprove, they will disapprove of your drinking and drug abuse rather than your honest admission that you need help.

convinced in your own mind that these feelings of worthlessness are unfounded. A word of warning here. Sometimes such feelings are so bound up with all sorts of childhood hurts and damaging adult experiences that this is not a job for a well-meaning amateur. There may be such deeply ingrained emotions at work that they can be worked through only with a trained, qualified, and experienced professional. A doctor is a good first port of call to decide whether such treatment is necessary and, if so, counsellors, psycho-therapists, and psychologists are on hand to provide specialist help.

Close friends and partners can also help. If shame is not so acute but general feelings of worthlessness are dragging you down, you can try the following. Draw up a list (or draw one up with a partner or close friend) of all the good points in your character. Are you kind, funny, helpful or considerate? Before the addiction took hold, did you play with the children, share the housework, or plan surprises? You now have, in black and white, factual evidence that your feelings are misleading you and that you are a much better person than you are letting yourself believe. The list might look something like the one opposite.

In privacy and in confidence take the time to blow your own trumpet. Take credit for all the positive aspects of your character and write them down so that you have the evidence to prove you are not the bad person you might feel you are. Then, again on the principle that doing something is better than worrying, set yourself different goals to achieve; goals that reinforce the positive facets of your character. Each one will help to reverse the direction of the downward spiral that's sapping your confidence and determination.

Feelings vs facts

I feel as if I'm unlovable, but I must remind myself that:

- My children love me.
- I have lots of friends.
- My wife/husband loves me.

I feel inadequate. I must remind myself that:

- I'm good at my work.
- I take pride in my job.
- I try to be a good parent.

I feel useless, but I must remember that:

- I'm humorous/clever/good company.
- I'm good at sewing, singing, putting up shelves, DIY.

Learning to manage fear

We keep saying that it takes courage to do what you are doing; and we'll carry on saying it. You're confronting a demon, slaying a dragon. This means that, in one way or another, you're facing your own personal fears. No wonder you feel nervous about whether you'll go the distance.

The key to managing fear is not to get too terrified. Concentrate on the step you're taking now rather becoming anxious about the road ahead. At the time you may feel as if you're moving so slowly that you're not really getting anywhere at all, but the steps add up, and taken together they lead to real progress.

Another way to manage fear is to talk about it. Acknowledge that the fear is the first stage in the process of dealing with it and talk openly and honestly about it – this will take away some of its sting. It may have been fear that drove you to addiction in the first place: fear of dealing with pain, loss, bereavement, failure. You escaped temporarily from the painful realities of life and took comfort in the seductive but ultimately empty promises of the bottle. Now you've decided to throw away the bottle, those fears will start crowding in again. You have more to contend with: fear and the fear of fear. It's not easy!

This may be the time to share your burden with someone else. Sharing your experiences with people who've had similar experiences can be an enormous reassurance and comfort. Sharing your fears with a loved one can also help but, under the right circumstances, it can do far more besides. It can also deepen a relationship far more than you ever thought possible, taking you both to a deeper level of trust and intimacy.

However, if your fears are too paralysing and disturbing, think about seeking professional help from counsellors who can explore your own circumstances more deeply. They are likely to have seen similar cases and there's nothing you can say that will surprise or shock them. Counsellors, doctors, nurses, and medical professionals of all kinds are only human; **they will understand, not judge**.

Learning to manage isolation

Recovering from addiction can be a lonely state of affairs. Nobody understands quite what you're going through and anyone who says, 'I understand how you're feeling' almost certainly doesn't. This can lead to a sense of isolation; as if you're locked in your own bubble of pain watching the world going on its merry way without you.

If this is the case, ask yourself honestly whether you weren't just as lonely when you were hooked on your own particular 'poison'. When you were high or drunk or betting like someone possessed were you really taking part in life or were you just escaping from it? In fact, you were probably just as lonely then as you feel now, but you just weren't aware of it. The addiction would have pushed you further and further from people into your own personal cocoon of isolation. Now, however, although you may sometimes feel lonely, you have an opportunity to get to know people and to join in with everything life has to offer.

This can take some time and effort. After all, you've lost many of your social skills during the years of addiction. Yet they will soon come back.

In the first instance, you can get a lot of support from the people at organizations like Alcoholics Anonymous. They will help you through the difficult days and months ahead and, although they will not know 'how you feel', they will have similar experiences to swap and advice to give.

You must resist going back to your old drinking, betting or drug-using pals. It may seem like they are the only ones who really know what you're going through but, unless they've made the brave decision you have to stay sober or clean, they don't. They are still in their separate world of addiction and they simply won't understand the heroic efforts you are trying to make. You may have to resign yourself to losing old friends in order to gain new ones who will not drag you back into your old ways. As ever, the choice is yours. The same old ways and the same dead end with nothing to hope for, or a new life with its endless possibilities.

A word for carers

Much of the above section has been directed at the addict. If you are the partner or the parent of that person, bear in mind the jumble of emotions at work. These emotions will also take their toll on you; not for nothing has alcoholism been called a family disease, for example.

Carers, too, are prone to many of the emotions described above. Many suffer guilt and anxiety or anger and uncertainty. A carer can be constantly on edge, turning the door key with dread as they wonder in what state they will find their partner. Such instability can lead to depression, sleeplessness, and a long-term despair that they will never be a 'normal' family again.

There are two basic ways to support an alcoholic. Both can be motivated by love, but one is negative and the other positive. Let's look at the negative one first.

Too supportive

The partner can be so supportive that at times it almost seems that he or she is actually colluding in the addiction. Partners will phone the office to make excuses for absences, take all the responsibility for running the home, paying the bills and cleaning the house while, for example, the alcoholic continues to drink, blithely unaware of all the responsibilities being avoided.

Partners will convince themselves against all the evidence that the addiction is essentially under control and that everything in the household is normal. For instance, they will tidy away bottles and cans, dispose of them discreetly, and give every impression to neighbours and friends that all is fine and dandy, even persuading themselves that there is nothing to worry about.

Paradoxically, some of these carers can find themselves deeply troubled if their partner suddenly stops drinking and tries for a cure. All at once they find that their own role of carer and protector no longer exists. Many also find that they have been subconsciously blaming everything that was wrong with their life on their partner's drinking. When that excuse suddenly disappears, they have to look at some of the personal problems in their own life and start, sometimes painfully, to take responsibility for them. In some cases, the carer can actively resent the fact that their alcoholic partner is making a recovery. Far better, they reason, to have the old life back where the alcoholic was totally dependent on them.

Honesty

The positive way to care involves 'tough love', 'being cruel to be kind', 'the carrot and the stick'. This means facing the problem honestly and not cushioning the alcoholic from the consequences of a behaviour and lifestyle that will ultimately kill. It means persuading the addict to seek treatment and, in the face of repeated resistance, honestly asking whether your and your children's well-being is ultimately served by remaining in an alcoholic household. While neither advocating nor condemning divorce or separation, we're saying that these terrible and painful questions need to be asked and that the full implications of an addict's continued reluctance to seek help need to be fully and clearly known by all concerned.

This admittedly is a worst-case scenario and the likelihood that you are in this position is, we hope, still remote. Yet in moments of your partner's sobriety, it's worth discussing the bottom line. Just as it's good to encourage the drinker, the drug user, or the gambler that a better future is in reach if he or she quits, it's wrong to blind them to the possibility that an infinitely worse one awaits them if they don't. Only when we each recognize that our actions have consequences and that ultimately we alone take responsibility for them, will any cure have a chance of success.

Communication

One of the keys to helping someone resume a full and healthy life is communication. This is one of the basic human functions, and surprisingly so many of us are not very good at it. Talking something through rather than keeping it bottled up inside is the secret of well-being.

Establishing lifelines

Recovering addicts can't beat this terrible disease alone. It takes a whole community to provide the support and the care needed to bring someone from dependence to self-control. Doctors, counsellors, psychotherapists, voluntary organizations and friends and family are all part of that community, and it's best to seek out sympathetic people from across the spectrum to help yourself to get well.

Establish a network of 'safe houses' where you know there will be no temptation to hand and where the people are aware of your desire to quit your addiction. Ask whether, for a limited period (say a fortnight or a month), you can pop around for a chat if times are getting hard. Have a number of friendly and sympathetic individuals on hand so that you don't have to impose on them too frequently or for too long. Remember that when you get better you're going to want to resume normal relations with them and putting them under too heavy a strain may damage that possibility. Restrict the times you call around to the sociable hours of daylight, rather than crashing in unannounced in the middle of the night. Your supporters have to have a life, too!

Q. Does alcohol affect women differently?

A. Yes. In general, women have a lower tolerance of alcohol and are advised not to drink while pregnant.

You should also have some hardcore 'buddies' who you can phone at 2 a.m. if necessary to get you through a really difficult patch (see Part 5, Chapter 14). It's expecting a lot of friends to be able to fill this role, but the specialist organizations often put you in touch with individuals prepared to give you this one-to-one care. When you're better, you may find you're in demand to provide this service yourself!

Above all, try to establish a routine in your life to keep your mind off whatever it is that most threatens to drag you back. Having early nights is a good idea not only because you're more likely to wake up fresh and focused on the challenges ahead, but also because it reduces the length of the evening danger zone when cravings can be at their most acute. If you live on your own, treat yourself to an electric blanket. Seriously. You may not have a partner to snuggle up to for warmth, but at least you can have the prospect of a deliciously warm bed to look forward to. Try also to eat earlier in the evening to do away with the seductive 'cocktail' hour, and drink plenty of water both to reduce cravings and to flush out your system.

Exercise is important to regain the vitality you've lost to addiction and to make you fit for all that your new life has to offer. However, choose an exercise routine that you can sustain. Going to the gym simply may not be an option for you whereas regular walks may be. Take yourself off into the countryside at weekends to explore new walks and to treat yourself to a change of scenery.

Try to take it easy and to do things calmly and in moderation. Going to the gym five nights a week is likely to be a bad idea. For one thing, you could burn yourself out and decide you're going to give up on the whole idea of exercise, or you might find yourself becoming hooked on the exercise and effectively swapping one addiction for another.

Take pleasure in the simple things of life unclouded by the fog of drugs or alcohol. Put like that, overcoming addiction sounds dead easy, but we're under no illusion that things are that simple. How many times have we said things like, 'Right. No chocolate after Christmas!' or 'I'm going on a diet. I'll start on Monday' only to be munching a bar of chocolate by New Year or finding reasons to put off the diet until the following Tuesday? If giving up chocolate and

---

MYTH: Drinking alcohol raises body temperature.

FACT: Drinking lowers rather than raises body temperature. Alcohol causes the blood vessels on the surface of your body to dilate and fill with more warm blood, creating the illusion of increased heat, but in fact the core (or central) body temperature decreases.

---

going on a diet are hard enough, we certainly appreciate the difficulties facing an addict making a new start. It's hard – possibly the hardest thing you've had to face. Yet take heart; the rewards will be the sweetest you've ever known.

Rediscover, if you can, the hobbies and interests that you had before you let them slide under the pressure of addiction, and consider learning new ones. Visit the library or the local adult education centre to see what courses are on offer. It needn't cost a fortune and concessions are available for those in financial straits. At no time in our history have so many educational opportunities been open to people. There are courses in everything from furniture making to beekeeping, from floristry to yoga, and from cake decoration to woodcarving open to all adults. **Go on. Give it a try.** Life's great. It would be a shame to sleep through it.

Planning the way ahead

If you're serious about quitting (and you must be because you're still reading!) you will discover to your surprise and perhaps initial dismay that you now have a future. Before, the future stretched only as far as the next drink, fix, or bet. Now that the future is infinite, knowing how you're going to fill it may be a daunting prospect.

The activities described above – the exercise, the hobbies and the night classes – are all practical things you can do in the early stages of recovery as a means of taking your mind off other things. Try now to see them as long-term pursuits that have a value in themselves. We're not saying you should start thinking of a career as a professional beekeeper or open a florist's shop, but rather that you should think of whatever you do as a positive end in itself and something that's directed at getting you back into the mainstream of life. It may not be an evening class or anything specifically to do with hobbies or leisure pursuits of any kind; it may simply be taking pleasure in the joys and responsibilities of everyday life.

You may think it's time you started to visit your relatives a little more often or that you started to patch up a family feud or help out at the local community centre. Don't look too far ahead just yet, but at least start considering that your future may stretch more than a few hours ahead of you.

For so long now you've led a totally self-centred life. That's not a judgement on you, just a fact. All you could see, all you cared about, all you really wanted was that all too brief illusion of well-being that would take you away from the difficult realities of life. Everyone and everything else was an irrelevance to you. Now you've woken up to the realization that your needs aren't the only ones in the world. What about the needs of your long suffering partner, your elderly parents, or your children? What about your friends? Start to think of them now.

In short, begin to consider others and you will discover a whole new practical and emotional dimension to life. It's not just the doing of things (vital though that is) but the connection with others that makes us truly human. This is an aspect of life that addicts tragically deny themselves – not because they don't want this connection but because they don't know how to make it. They simply cannot see beyond their own physical needs in the moment. Yet an addict's moments are essentially sterile; they are all exactly the same and endlessly repeated to no long-term purpose whereas each moment you are sober or clean belongs to a series of moments that gradually accumulates into a full and productive life. Perhaps you're reading this on a good day. Great. You're feeling that bit stronger, more focused and determined to look beyond your own self into a future you can share with others. We wish you well. With hard work and determination and a good support system of friends, you can beat addiction in the end.

However, maybe this has not been such a good week at all and you're feeling like throwing in the towel already. Please try to hang in there – for your sake and your future – and realize in your head, if not yet in your heart that there is a better life out there. In Part 3, we look at practical steps to take if you're feeling low or prey to temptation, but for the moment try to be firm and know that even the longest nights eventually give way to daytime. It's early days yet, so take it easy, step by step.

Part 2: Taking the Next Steps

There's a story that's particularly appropriate to your situation at the moment. It's about a young boy anxiously awaiting his first day at primary school and resentfully contemplating an end to his carefree time at home with Mum.

'Do I have to go to school, Mum?' he asks gloomily.
'Yes,' she explains, 'everybody does but you'll like it once you get there.'
'I'd rather stay here with you,' he replies, unconvinced.
'I know,' she adds reassuringly, 'but you'll make lots of new friends.'
'I don't need new friends. I like it here at home with you.'

The summer passes and the big day arrives. The boy's mother takes him to school and, wiping a tear from her eye, leaves him at the gate on the brink of this new phase in his life.

Come 3.30 p.m. the mother is back at the gate surprised and delighted to see her son running out of the playground full of smiles.
'You were right, Mum. It wasn't so bad after all,' he says, 'but I'm glad it's all over. Now we can get back to normal.'

There may be something in that boy's experience that strikes a chord with you right now. You've made the heroic effort to admit to your addiction and to do something about it. Perhaps at this point you've not had a drink or a bet for a couple of weeks and you're thinking, 'Right then. That's it. Sorted. Back to normal.' It's only now beginning to dawn on you that actually it isn't. Just as the young boy would have to be told that school wasn't a one-day affair but a long-term process, so you're beginning to realize that your recovery is going to be an ongoing commitment. 'Can I hack it?' you wonder.

Well, the answer is yes, you can, just as hundreds of thousands have done before you. And that's what we hope this part of the book will do: namely persuade you to hang on in there. The process of healing *has* begun. By the end of this section we hope you'll have the confidence and self-awareness to believe you *are* slowly getting better.

This doesn't stop you feeling a sudden sense of dread that, far from reaching its end, the journey has only just begun. Have you ever struggled up a hill, seeing the summit coming tantalizingly into view, only to discover that it's not the summit after all, but that there's another ridge stretching up beyond it? This is possibly how you feel now. It's difficult, but stay the course, go the distance and **you will reach the top**.

One way to get over that niggling sense of anticlimax is to take the credit for all you have done. Pat yourself on the back for all the strides and changes you've made, and all the positive achievements you've racked up. It really is something to feel proud of. With every day that passes your strength and determination will grow.

Now do an audit of the practical benefits that have come your way since you decided to turn your life around. Make a list and include them all – small or large – from the fact that you don't smell of alcohol all day to the fact that you've rediscovered some of the simple joys of family life. When the going threatens to get tough, read through this list and take quiet and much deserved satisfaction from it.

Nonetheless, be prepared for the occasional hard knock which will bring you up sharp just when you thought you were doing so well. For instance, doesn't it feel good to have more money in your pocket (or at least to see your debts going down)? Doesn't it feel good to wake in the morning with a clear head or to get through the afternoon without the fog of painkillers or sleeping pills? Doesn't it feel good to get control back in your life rather than to be at the mercy of your old destructive behaviour? Yes, it does. Yet come 7 p.m. when friends are gathering in the pub or you're considering a large scotch and soda with just the soda, the lure of the old life can sometimes seem irresistible. 'Just one proper drink won't do any harm', you think, in fact, I actually *need* a drink because the temptation is unbearable. And besides, after all I've put myself through I've earned it.'

This is the time for the cognitive approach – let your head do the talking rather than allow your feelings to call the shots (see page 71). You *know* deep down that 'just the one' will undo all the good work you've put in up to this point. So hang on to that thought despite the terrible strain you'll be going through.

In Part 3 we suggest practical approaches to deal with temptation (see Chapter 9), but for now let us say this: we know that what you're going through is hard. No, we don't know exactly what you, personally, are going through or how you're feeling – nobody but you will ever know that – but we understand from the men and women we've spoken to over the years that it's tough. Probably the toughest thing you've ever had to confront in your life, and we salute your efforts.

The Russian writer, Alexander Solzhenitsyn, describing the terrible conditions in Stalin's prison camps in Siberia once wrote that a man who is warm cannot possibly imagine what it is like to be cold. The same applies to your situation. People who've never been in the grip of addiction can't possibly know what it feels like to suffer post-addiction cravings. However, to get as far as you've got is a real achievement – be proud of it, and get yourself ready for the next stage of your recovery.

4

Taking stock

By now you will probably have located and listed the organizations that can offer you help (you'll find a full list in Part 6), but you may not have plucked up the confidence to contact them yet. That, we would suggest, is the next step. Don't be afraid or embarrassed. The people there have seen it all before and most of them will probably have personal experience of what you're going through so there's nothing you can say that will shock or surprise them. On the contrary, you'll receive level-headed advice from people willing you to get better.

Practical lifelines

Once you have made contact with a group, they can then become your advisers, friends, supporters, champions and counsellors. They'll be there in a crisis or during a moment of weakness to encourage you to carry on, and they will do so without judgement or blame. What's more, going along to talk to strangers will take some of the strain off family members who, don't forget, are going through their own problems too. You'll begin to realize the truth of the old saying, 'A problem shared is a problem halved.' Of course, getting used to talking about personal problems may come as a bit of a shock for some. Perhaps you are the type of person who keeps emotions bottled up and rarely talks openly about the deep things that are on your mind. If so, give it a try. We guarantee you will be amazed at how helpful talking can be. It doesn't cost a penny, and it's one of the simplest, most effective forms of therapy there is.

In most cases, however, a talking cure alone is not enough. Many alcoholics or drug abusers will need medical intervention from the day it becomes clear that drug or alcohol dependency has reached a critical stage. A controlled programme of detoxification may be required before the underlying causes of addiction can be addressed. It's vital to stress that detoxification (or 'detox' as it's more widely known) should only be carried out under qualified medical supervision.

MYTH: Willpower alone will cure most addictions. It's just a matter of giving up.

FACT: Determination and will are vital in the long-term treatment of addiction but alone they will not solve the problem. By the time people have developed a pattern of addictive behaviour, they have begun to be psychologically and physically dependent on a substance. Simply giving up is not enough; they need to be supported by professionals who can understand and deal with a complex web of need.

Drug and alcohol detoxification

What is detox?

Detox is the first stage in the treatment of acute alcohol and drug abuse. It involves the controlled and gradual removal of harmful substances from the body and dramatically increases the chances of long-term rehabilitation being effective. While still under the influence of drugs or alcohol, an addict will simply not be in the appropriate state of mind to take part in the demanding processes of long-term treatment.

Detox can be carried out over a period of days or weeks either as an in-patient in a hospital or clinic, or at home under proper supervision. Simply stopping can have disastrous consequences on a person's health, prompting withdrawal symptoms such as:

- Headaches

- Vomiting

- Delirium Tremens (tremors known as the shakes or DTs)

- Seizures

- Profuse sweating

- Palpitations

- Diarrhoea

- Insomnia

- Depression

- Anxiety

- Confusion

- Stomach and muscle cramps.

It is essential to consult your doctor for guidance about how to best proceed with an appropriate detox programme. You may be able to get treatment on the National Health Service (NHS) or you may be referred to one of the many private clinics providing a drug and alcohol detox service.

MYTH: Drinking a pint of milk before drinking alcohol stops you getting drunk.

FACT: Drinking milk or eating food beforehand does not prevent absorption of alcohol into the blood but it will slow the process down. It will not stop you getting drunk if you drink to excess.

What to expect from a residential detox programme

Treatment centres are designed to be non-threatening so don't expect a cold, unwelcoming establishment where you will be treated like some sort of deviant. Private centres look for all the world like rather upmarket hotels, where the staff are on hand to help you in any way they can, but don't expect to have a holiday while you're there. These centres exist to provide professional clinical and psychological care, and some of the things the staff tell you may make for uncomfortable listening.

NHS detox centres may not always be so glamorous (although they can be), but they will essentially provide the same friendly, non-threatening environment, a relaxed but professional atmosphere and, crucially, the same standard of medical care and supervision.

The first day is taken up with an assessment of your situation and your likely needs in the future. If you are dependent on alcohol you may experience some of the above withdrawal symptoms several hours after your last drink. This can be very unpleasant and you may need medical help to relieve the symptoms.

On admission to the centre, you may be

prescribed a course of tablets to reduce the severity of the withdrawal and to tide you over until your system physically adjusts itself to an alcohol-free state. The tablets are essentially designed to lessen the discomfort of withdrawal and to prevent you from having a fit, which may occur if you suddenly stop drinking without medical supervision, having drunk large amounts for a long period of time. In addition, you are likely to be prescribed vitamins (particularly vitamin B) that are designed to help repair the damage alcohol may have caused to your central nervous system and to prevent any problems occurring with your memory.

The detox process can take up to a week during which time you may suffer from insomnia and feelings of anxiety accompanied by moderate or profuse sweating. This is perfectly normal and is the body's way of readjusting to its normal functions after years of excess and abuse. Be reassured that the symptoms will decrease in severity and even the cravings will be manageable. When the detox is complete, the body is physically ready for the second stage in the rehabilitation process: a thorough mental self-examination.

It is rare for a week's detox to be sufficient to end an alcoholic lifestyle. In the vast majority of cases, a lengthy course of therapy and counselling is needed to address the reasons behind alcohol addiction. Only then will you be in a position to avoid relapsing into your old ways.

Detox at home

Home detox is *not* DIY (do-it-yourself) detox. An addict *cannot* do this alone and needs the back-up of a trained healthcare professional. In most ways, the procedure is similar to that provided in a residential centre, differing only in that it is structured around the individual's domestic routines. Those opting for this method find it offers them both the medical support they need combined with the minimum disruption to normal family life. They find they can maintain contact with family and friends while benefiting from the highest standards of clinical supervision.

Twenty-four hour nursing cover will normally be provided for an agreed period of time, followed by reduced cover as the recovering addict improves. During this time, a specific treatment plan will be drawn up and the patient given clear information about what this treatment will involve.

Once the detox is complete and the body has returned to an alcohol- or drug-free state, the person is ready for the next and longer term stage of recovery: that all-important mental re-think.

What is rehab?

Rehab (short for 'rehabilitation') is the umbrella term for the gradual process of recovery from addiction. Alcoholism cannot be cured, but it can be successfully treated and managed. Those who've stopped using drugs or alcohol are frequently referred to as 'recovering' addicts.

It is important to stress that rehab is a long-term process and even a lengthy stay in a residential centre will not necessarily solve the problem in one stroke. In fact, it's probably better talking about living with the problem rather than solving it. The rehab process can begin in a centre or it can begin at home – it can even begin with a book like this – but ultimately it will have to be carried out against the daily backdrop of everyday life.

> **MYTH:** *Slot machines are more likely to pay out after a long run of no shows and near misses.*
>
> **FACT:** Slot machines pay out on a completely random basis. Those who claim to detect a pattern are fooling themselves.

The next stage for problem gamblers

Problem gambling is a less visible addiction than alcoholism or drug abuse but it is just as damaging to mental well-being and personal relationships. People gamble for a variety of reasons. For some, it is the buzz of living on the edge or the excitement of a big win teamed with the danger of a catastrophic loss. For others, it is an escape from the pain of difficult situations. Either way, it appears to offer short-term relief from the pressures of reality, but in fact it only adds to the pressures.

Although there are no physical withdrawal symptoms when a person stops gambling, there are mental and psychological stresses that can manifest themselves in physical ways. A person can be subject to noticeable mood swings or experience bouts of anxiety, depression or irritability. He or she might find it difficult to sleep or might lose the appetite for food – or even start to eat excessively.

After gamblers have admitted their need for help and taken the first practical steps to reorder their finances, they need to begin the gradual process of recovery by seeking advice from one of the recognized organizations such as Gamblers Anonymous.

Gambling is frequently a solitary addiction, despite the real but ultimately sterile camaraderie of the betting shop or the casino. The gambler has to hide the excitement of a win or the disappointment of a loss from family and friends so as not to reveal the true extent of dependency. And as gamblers will be spending increasing amounts of time and mental energy on their addiction, it means they will have correspondingly less energy to spend on their families. Isolated in their own bubble of addictive behaviour, they are cut off from all the normal pleasures and strains of life. As a result, often they will be incapable of either sharing the pleasures or summoning the concentration to shoulder the stresses. Little wonder that family relationships – let alone the bank balance – suffer tremendously.

MYTH: An occasional gambling binge is harmless.

FACT: Most gamblers say that however 'occasional' their gambling, the periods in between binges are characterized by anticipation of the next one. This in turn leads them to become morose, nervous or irritable with potentially damaging implications for human relationships.

Recovery involves rebuilding relationships and learning to live as a contributing member of a family or a society. The role of the counsellor or therapist in the gambling rehabilitation process is to help the addict to understand the root cause of his or her dependency and to recognize the danger signs that could trigger a return to problem gambling. The treatment typically involves individual counselling and group therapy in addition to education both for the gambler and for his or her family. The effectiveness of the treatment depends on the commitment of each individual, but studies have shown abstinence rates reaching nearly 60 per cent one year after a treatment programme.

5

Changing the patterns of your life

If you have spent a large proportion of your life as an addict, you will know that suddenly removing the object of your addiction leaves you feeling strangely adrift. Since every waking hour was spent feeding your addiction or thinking about it, you suddenly find now you are sober or clean, that you appear to have lost all purpose in life. This is quite a natural response, but it is a complete illusion. In reality, you now have the possibility to discover the real point of life and to reintroduce into your life the purpose that drinking, gambling or using drugs had siphoned away. Time for the cognitive approach – listen to reason and do not be fooled by sensation (see page 71).

Take control

Think of yourself in a car. You can sit in the back seat and let your destructive behaviour take you where it leads. You can abandon all responsibility for the trip and be content to end up where alcoholism and drug abuse finally dump you when the juice runs out. Or you can climb into the driver's seat and take control of the whole journey. You may slow down here or speed up there, but essentially you have both hands on the wheel and you are taking full charge of the route.

It takes time and effort to readjust. Taking control of your life after being so long out of control isn't easy. However, we hope you realize it's a prize worth winning. Give it your best shot; you have nothing to lose and everything to gain. Draw up a list of your new priorities, it may read something like this:

- Avoid your old haunts

- Tell your friends your intentions

- Renew your old interests

- Develop new interests

- Start helping others

- Help your partner

- Get up if you fall

- Set achievable goals

- Make new friends.

Avoid your old haunts

Don't put yourself in places that will lead you into temptation. Avoid pubs, bars, clubs, betting shops, dog tracks or casinos even though you think you can go along merely as a spectator or to meet your old mates. If you've been a gambler, resist the temptation to pick up the sports pages and check the racing results. In time, even as a recovering alcoholic, you will be able to go into a pub with friends and be content to chat over a coke or a tonic, but in the early stages of abstinence don't put yourself in situations that could trigger a relapse.

Tell your friends your intentions

Make it clear to friends and colleagues that you're serious about making a life change. Most will know that you have had a problem, and while some will applaud and support you in your efforts to change, others will try to scupper your good intentions either deliberately or out of ignorance. Tempting you to have 'just the one' or to go to the races are not the actions of a true friend. If they continue to encourage you to drink, bet or use drugs as you used to do, the time has come for you to part company. True friends work with you for your well-being and do not aid and abet your destruction.

Renew your old interests

What gave you pleasure before you were an addict? Doing DIY about the house, dressmaking, gardening and going down to the garden centre, planning the summer holiday with the kids, window shopping on Saturday and stopping off for tea in the afternoon? Write a list of all the things you used to do before your priorities switched, and start to rediscover the pleasure you took in them.

Develop new interests

You are really starting with a clean slate now, and many things you may never have dreamed of are suddenly possible if you give them a go. Take up new hobbies and leisure pursuits or, if you're not the type for carpentry, embroidery or beekeeping, take pleasure in the simple things like walking, talking and seeing the world through eyes unclouded by harmful substances.

Start helping others

Don't be a victim. Don't sit down passively and wait for things to happen when you could use your life experience to help others. Share your story with others and, for example, at Alcoholics Anonymous meetings, take the initiative in opening yourself up to the group. Helping others is a surefire way to take the focus off yourself and your problems.

Charities are always looking for helping hands. Write, phone, or go along in person to see whether you have the skills they could use. Deliver the local free newspaper, help out one afternoon a week in the charity shop, visit the elderly or the housebound, join in your local church or community centre, become involved in the village hall – do anything that keeps you active, focused, and able to regain a sense of the purpose you thought you'd lost.

Help your partner

Charity begins at home. Don't make the quite common and natural mistake of putting so much effort into your 'new' life that you start to neglect the old one. Many people often swap one obsession (drink or drugs) for another (doing good works), and in effect begin to substitute one form of addiction for another. They become oblivious to the fact that, whereas alcohol and gambling were driving them to neglect their partner and family, excessive 'busy-ness' is now having exactly the same effect. Learn to be attentive and considerate to your partner. We're not talking candlelit meals and long stemmed roses, but perhaps offering to do the shopping, the washing or the ironing while your partner relaxes with a magazine. Offer to run a bath or to make a cup of tea for them without being asked.

Your decision to kick your destructive habits is opening up a new world where everything is possible. Even the most damaging behaviour can be turned into something positive. Life is not all plain sailing; it's about hard knocks too. If you can learn from the hard knocks (as you're probably beginning to do) and turn them around, you will find that the quality of your domestic and personal life will be enhanced immeasurably. If you and your partner go through this honestly and openly and support *each other* through it, you could find your relationship deepening and strengthening in a way you would never have imagined. This is one of the rewards of kicking the old addictions and, as before, it's a prize worth winning.

If you are single or live alone, you may find that by renewing friendships and putting effort into relationships that have lapsed you will get a better sense of purpose and belonging.

Get up if you fall

This is difficult because we don't want to suggest that falling off the wagon is inevitable or that relapsing isn't serious, but realistically it happens. Those on diets know exactly what the implications of breaking the rules are. You starve yourself for weeks then, in a moment of weakness, take a bite out of a Danish pastry and, before you can say 'Help', have polished off the lot and are eyeing up another one. You feel a guilty but delicious sense of pleasure followed by a momentary sense of disgust and shame, then (most damaging of all) the utter conviction that you'll never stick to a diet again so it's not even worth trying. This is a common mistake. If you fall, get up and resolve not to slip again. Don't wallow in the self pity; just say to yourself, 'I'm going to put this lapse behind me and not worry about it. And from now on I'll really try to stick to my guns and not let this happen again.'

Set achievable goals

Remember the list of goals you drew up in Part 1 (page 74)? Now's the time to take another look at it and revise it if necessary. Plan small, step-by-step changes in preference to the big master plan. Don't worry if they don't look all that impressive on paper, you're trying to steer yourself away from addiction so anything that takes your mind off your old habits will be worthwhile.

Make new friends

You'll probably find yourself gradually moving away from some of your old drinking or gambling mates the moment you decide to change your life. Some will want to drag you back into the old ways, and you may feel you're letting them down by avoiding them, but real friends will respect your decision to change and want the best for you. Keep the friends who will stand by you, and drop those who want to suck you back into their dangerous lifestyle. With all the new things you're beginning to do now, the chances are you'll be making new friends all the time. Think of this as a completely new start.

MYTH: My friend has got to get himself out of this mess on his own. There's nothing I can do.

FACT: You can help. Try to be honest with your friend and gently tell him or her there is a problem. Pretending to ignore it or sweeping it under the carpet is not what true friends are for. Gently suggest he seeks help and support him in his efforts.

A word for carers

In this section so far we've lavished all our praise on the addict who's decided to turn his or her life around. This is absolutely appropriate, but it's time now for a few words in praise of partners and friends whose patience, encouragement and support cannot be stressed enough.

You are the unsung heroes and heroines of all this, the ones waiting silently in the wings while the addict gets all the help and attention centre stage. All too often, your contribution to this healing process is overlooked as the addict takes all the credit for recovery. This includes all the sleepless nights you've spent wondering how you were going to keep house and home together, all the lonely evenings you spent not knowing at what time (and in what state) your partner was going to come home, and all the unreasonable demands someone else's addictive behaviour put on *your* life.

At times, it must have seemed that you simply didn't have a life, that your role and purpose were simply to look after someone who was selfishly putting their interests above everything else. You may have been working hard at a job – possibly two jobs – to make ends meet while all the time what little you earned was being siphoned off at the betting shop or the pub. You may have been trying to protect your children from your partner's terrible behaviour or holding the family together despite all the stresses and strains of addiction. Most of all, you may have been trying to maintain a loving relationship with someone who, hell bent on self-destruction, was rejecting you and everything you cherished. Well done for staying the course; you have our sincerest admiration. Next are some lifelines for you.

Don't blame yourself

The only people who can take the responsibility for addiction are the addicts themselves. In the end, the recovering alcoholic or the one-time gambler has to own up to the personal responsibility they bear for the situation they're in. There will be mitigating circumstances, there will be reasons, there will be terrible pressures that drove a person to the bottle or the needle but no one other than the addict took the decision to choose that course of action. This is grown-up stuff. Neither of you is a child anymore; you are both responsible for your own lives. No one else can carry that particular load. So, don't blame yourself. 'I should have done this', 'if only I'd done that, he/she wouldn't have gone off the rails, if only... if only...' No, none of these things apply. Perhaps you would do things differently if you had your time again, but no one is perfect. We may all start out wanting to be perfect wives and mothers, husbands and fathers, but none of us are. Moreover no one has the right to accuse you of not getting it right all of the time. Put very simply, all this mess is not your fault.

Accept that you can't wave a magic wand

There is only so much you can do. You are not Superman or Superwoman, and not even a partner you love has the right to expect you to be. Remember, these are grown-up matters where adults have to accept the responsibility for their own lives. We're talking tough love here. Of course, one partner will support the other through the hard times (don't you know it!), but an adult partnership depends on both parties behaving as fully responsible adults. There is no such thing as unconditional love in an adult relationship. It's a two-way street; love has to be earned and worked at.

You may want to say, 'There, there, don't worry. It'll be fine.' Just as you did reassuringly to your three-year-old child when she woke terrified in the night. But your partner is not a three-year-old child and you have to be prepared to face the possibility that things may not turn out fine. Be prepared to accept that the outcome of this terrible episode in your life is largely out of your hands.

We spoke earlier of crisis sometimes deepening a relationship. Sadly, it can also destroy it. This will make for gloomy reading, we know, but it happens. All you can do is give this your best shot and hope that your partnership survives. With commitment, communication, and plenty of give and take there's a strong possibility it will. Yet if the worst happens and you find an addict's pre- or post-recovery behaviour is impossible to bear, it will not have been your fault. Don't blame yourself for not being able to wave that magic wand.

Make time for yourself

You have a life, too. And you have the right to enjoy it. If you have got this far, you almost certainly haven't shirked your responsibilities as a carer. You haven't taken your partner's problems lightly, and you've probably worried yourself sick about how to put them right. So, now take a little time off.

Try to have at least half a day in the week to yourself. Possibly more. Make it a time when you do what you want to do as an individual without a care in the world (not easy, we know!). This may involve pampering yourself at the hairdressers, retreating to your greenhouse with a seed catalogue; meeting a friend for a gossip over a pub lunch, or taking yourself off for a walk in the country. Make that your special time, a time when you can just relax and recharge your batteries.

Think about getting a babysitter if necessary – not for an evening, when most couples are thinking about going out on the town, but for an afternoon when you just want to wander around a car boot sale or a farmers' market. This is a way of maintaining your sanity in what can be a chaotic situation.

Of course, if your partner looks like he or she is really on the mend, then get that babysitter so you can both enjoy some quality time. Or, better still, go out as a family and enjoy the time together. The point is that you should make the decision that **rest and relaxation are not luxuries but necessities**. Factor them into your joint *and personal* timetable.

Look after your health

One of you is sick. That's bad enough. Imagine what it would be like if both of you were. You must look after your health. You will be of no use to your partner if you are laid up in bed suffering from exhaustion. More importantly, you owe it to yourself to be healthy enough to enjoy your life to the full.

The keys to good health are diet and exercise. This doesn't mean lobster and fillet steak followed by a trip to the gym and the rowing machine. It's more straightforward than that – buy simple ingredients and cook them well rather than relying on ready meals and takeaways. If you're not a natural cook, buy a recipe book! You'll be amazed what you can do with potatoes, cheese, bacon, pasta and mince. And that's only for starters. There are hundreds of cookbooks geared towards simple, cheap and wholesome everyday food. Here's a tip: buy a Nigel Slater cookbook. His are among the tastiest, simplest and most down-to-earth recipes we know.

As we said earlier, exercise is not about dressing up in lycra and joining the gym. It's about walking, cycling, playing rounders in the park, kicking a ball about with the kids – just being active rather than passively staring at the television. Scientists have proved that taking exercise stimulates chemicals in the body that make us feel better. In other words, taking exercise isn't a dreary form of duty, it's a real boost to our mental and physical well-being. And goodness knows, you need to keep strong and healthy now more than ever.

Develop your own life

This is rather more than simply making time for yourself and taking yourself off once a week to a coffee shop in town while someone looks after the children. It's about an attitude of mind that says you have a right to live your own life rather than putting it on hold. Naturally, you will want to support your partner until their crisis is over, but we suggest that you will support your partner best in the long term not by suspending your own life or by subordinating it indefinitely to your partner's life, but by maintaining your own life simultaneously. That way, when the crisis is past, you can meet again on an equal footing – not as nurse and patient or carer and victim.

6

Caring for the children

Children are the innocent, vulnerable, and puzzled victims of a parent's addiction and they will need special care. It is sometimes said that alcoholism, for example, is a family illness – while only one person has the disease, everybody suffers the fall-out. As the addict organizes his or her life around an addiction, so the family organizes its life around the addict.

The National Association for the Children of Alcoholics (NACOA) (see page 302) has isolated the unspoken rules that develop in order to give the illusion of normality in an abnormal family setting. They are equally applicable to all forms of addiction.

- Don't talk
- Don't trust
- Don't feel.

In adults, these strategies would be a form of denial. In children lacking the maturity or the insight to understand the situation, they are merely methods of self-preservation and protection from what is the strange and unsettling behaviour of one (or both) of their parents.

In order to minimize the damage caused by an addictive parent, children should be helped to talk, trust and feel once again.

Talk

Communication is vital. Knowing what you're up against and having words to understand it are half the battle. Feeling unhappy and ill at ease is bad enough. Not knowing why you are feeling unhappy makes matters worse. And children suffer most in all of this. A parent needs to make it clear that there is a problem in the home, that it is not in the child's imagination, and that, under the circumstances, it is quite natural for that child to be upset. That's a start. If children are given this basic information, they will at least know that the problem isn't theirs and they will be less likely to blame themselves for it.

Then a parent can begin to name the problem and explain that the drinking, drug abusing, or gambling is an illnesses that everyone is working hard to try to cure. Remember that a child kept in the dark (but knowing something is wrong) will have a tendency to imagine or invent a scenario far worse than the real one. You may think you are being kind by saying nothing but in actual fact your silence could be making matters worse.

Try not to have rows in front of the children. If you have to have sharp words with a partner, do it when the children are out of the house.

Angry, raised voices will undermine the sense of normality you are trying to foster in the home and will make already fragile children more nervous.

Trust

An alcoholic or a drug abuser cannot be relied upon. He or she is guided only by the next drink, the next fix or the next tranquilizer. Everything and everyone else is secondary. Therefore, it will be left to you to build the frameworks on which a child can rely.

Only make promises to the children that you know you can keep. Rather than saying that you'll all go away on a fabulous camping holiday (only to find when the time comes that there's a problem with money) scale down your plans and say you'll all go to the swimming pool on Saturday and follow it with a barbecue. The most ordinary days out are often the best treats of all. Tell the children that you're all going on a picnic in the country and you need help to plan it all. Get the kids involved in making the sandwiches, packing the bats and balls, then set off in convoy for the train or bus station as if you're going on a Magical Mystery Tour. Your enthusiasm will be infectious and they will learn that normal happy family life is still possible in what are temporarily distressing circumstances. Seeing you happy will make them feel secure, and confident that they have a loving, functioning, and strong parent to take charge of them.

Promising treats and delivering them are the best ways of restoring trust in children. They will probably have resigned themselves to being let down so many times that they don't dare get their hopes up. Seeing you make a plan and stick to it is the first step on the road to self-confidence.

Treats aside, introduce the same sort of reliable structure into your children's everyday routine. Make sure they are up in good time for school, that they have a good breakfast, that they know what the arrangements for after school are and that you eat together as a family at a set time every evening. The ritual of shared meals is so important for functioning well as a family. It doesn't have to be the best bone china with napkins and cut-glass decanters; the food and the setting are unimportant. What is important is that you sit around your kitchen table together and enjoy each other's company.

If work or domestic commitments make this difficult, think about reinstating the Sunday lunch. Try to have at least one meal in the week that is special, a meal in which everybody has a role to play. Younger kids will love the involvement and even surly teenagers can be persuaded to lend a hand when they discover that the communal meal will be worthwhile and enjoyable. There is no better place to air family issues, discuss family tensions, and just have fun as a family than around the meal table. If you haven't done it yet, give it a try.

Feel

Once you have established lines of communication and introduced a framework of trust, you'll probably find your children opening up more to you, expressing their feelings, and telling you what's on their minds. In this way, you can deal with their emotional needs and have a better idea about what they're going through.

You might need to work a little harder with teenagers who are at that age when communication with parents is difficult anyway. Just be patient, don't take their rebuffs personally, and keep in there, constantly making it clear that you will be there for them when they need you. Try not to nag them too much about the state of their room or the shortness of their dress or whatever.

Instead, gently suggest why you think they should do this or that and treat them as adults involved in a two-way conversation.

Once children know that they have the freedom and confidence to talk about what's on their minds they will realize that, however chaotic one aspect of family life is, there is at least some safe space for them to carry on as normal. Creating that framework of trust is the best present you could give them.

Reassurance

Addiction is an immensely complex subject that is bewildering enough for the professionals. For children, it's virtually impossible to understand, and their parent's strange behaviour can seem very frightening. Consequently, they need constant reassurance that everyone is doing what they can to get things back to normal. Make sure you tell your children that:

- Addiction to drink or drugs is a disease. As a result of that disease their mother or father will sometimes say and do things that he or she would not normally do. It is not that they are bad people but just that the disease makes them lose control.

- The disease can be treated and everyone is doing their best to make sure that happens.

- They cannot control their parent's addiction and the addiction itself is not their fault.

- They are not the only ones going through this. The National Society for the Prevention of Cruelty to Children (NSPCC) estimates there are up to one million children in Britain living with parents who have a serious alcohol problem.

- They can talk to you about the problem whenever they like. Failing that, they should talk to someone they feel safe and comfortable with – an older brother or sister, perhaps, or a friend's parent or a teacher.

Preventative advice for parents

If your family has a history of alcoholism or if a parent is an alcoholic or heavy drinker, research suggests that your children will have a greater risk of a drinking problem in later life themselves. That, coupled with the greater accessibility of alcohol and the virtual encouragement of heavy drinking as a necessary component of a good night out, means that our youngsters are increasingly vulnerable.

You need to give your children advice soon. Start talking before they start drinking. This means setting an example from the moment they're born. Maintain open lines of communication and explain the importance of drinking in moderation. It's a good idea to get to know your children's friends, to have them all over for suppers and parties where drink is not the focal point and, without prying, find out where they're going when they go out.

Talking openly about drugs is also important. If you brush the issue under the carpet or seem embarrassed to raise it, children will miss out on important advice. Contrary to the impression they like to give, teenagers *do* listen to their parents. They won't always let on, but they will recognize at some level that the advice from people who care for them is in a different category from the drink and drugs education they may get from a visiting stranger at school. The child who can tell you that they have been offered drugs and who knows you won't hit the roof is less likely to take them in the first place. How often do you hear the phrase, 'I couldn't tell my dad. He'd go ballistic'?

Unfortunately, by the time you read this such preventative advice may be a little late. A problem drinker in the family may have set the wrong example already and perhaps you have not been comfortable discussing such sensitive issues. However, it really is never too late to learn. Be open and honest with your children. Choose your moment carefully so that what you say isn't overshadowed by other distractions. Set aside some time at the weekend, for example, when you know everyone will have time to open up. Never underestimate the value of the three C's: communication, communication, communication.

MYTH: There is little parents can do to stop their children experimenting with drugs and alcohol.

FACT: Parents are the most powerful influence on their children's behaviour, but leaving it until the child is already dabbling is too late. Influence is exerted by a lifetime of loving and open communication and by the strong reinforcement of parental example.

Q. Is alcoholism a disease?

A. Yes. It is a chronic disease characterized by an inability to control your drinking.

7

Taking control:
Emotional lifelines

In Chapters 5 and 6, we suggested some practical things you might like to consider in order to move to the next stage of your recovery. In this chapter, we look at some of the emotional matters you might want to deal with.

As we mentioned earlier, you're probably experiencing a jumble of emotions right now ranging from guilt and shame to fear and uncertainty. Yet you may not think of your present state in emotional terms at all. You may just feel an overwhelming sense of awfulness and depression about the fact that you've got yourself into this mess in the first place.

All these feelings are completely unhelpful to your recovery. What's more, these feelings essentially belong to the past. The guilt and shame about what you've done relates to past behaviour and not to your present circumstances. On the contrary, what you are doing now is courageous and positive. You've taken the bold and difficult decision to change the pattern of your life and to seek help for your problems. This is to be applauded wholeheartedly. Try as you might, you will not be able to change the past. What you can do is make adjustments in the present and eventually change the future.

We suggest that you take all the negative emotions and substitute each one for a positive emotion. The negative emotions, remember, belong to the past; the positive emotions are the emotional lifelines that will influence your future.

Responsibility not guilt

Guilt is not part of your recovery but personal responsibility is. Of course, you will have your 'off days' when all you can think about is what might have been. You will regret the things that hurt your partner or children. You will feel haunted by the money you squandered at the betting shop or in the online casino. You'll feel haunted by the wasted evenings spent with the bottle or the drugs and you'll find it hard to get those distressing images out of your mind.

This is where the cognitive approach comes into its own again (see page 71). Try to forget how you feel and, instead, try to concentrate on the positive steps you've taken. Take out all those lists again, make new ones, and set down all your achievements in black and white. Then, when you're prey to damaging feelings, you will know in your head that there's another side to the story. It's time to get into the driving seat and take control of your life once again. Take personal responsibility for your health. Decide you're going to eat and exercise sensibly and think about drawing up a personal fitness plan. Nothing elaborate, just a schedule outlining how much walking you intend to do or how many times you plan to go swimming. Why not set yourself targets – say, 50 lengths swimming a week or 8 km (5 miles) walking? You could even do a Jamie Oliver and work out a weekly menu – rewarding yourselves with a roast or a fry-up at the weekend.

Take personal responsibility for your finances and resolve not to squander money again. With your partner or with a friend, draw up a simple family budget with income in one column and expenditure in another. What savings can you make? Can you take sandwiches to work three days a week rather than eat in the canteen? Can you do without the cappuccino mid-afternoon, can you walk or cycle to work?

Take personal responsibility for every aspect of your recovery and tell yourself repeatedly that you are determined not to go back to your old ways. Make responsible decisions about the people you will associate with, and the places you will (or will not) visit. Take life seriously as if every day was your last. As a gambler, a drug abuser, or an alcoholic you were content for life to happen to you. **Now start to control it**. It's your life after all; nobody else can live it for you.

Pride not shame

So, you got yourself into some pretty bad states in the past. Stop dwelling on them and start concentrating on the positive things you've done. Take pride in your achievements, however small. Deciding to come off drugs or alcohol or to give up gambling is your own personal Everest and you have every right to feel justifiably proud.

Take pride in becoming a properly functioning mother or father again. Start to rediscover the simple joys and responsibilities of family life. Don't think of yourself as a victim but as a person who, against all the odds, is trying to build a new life. Learn from your mistakes and resolve not to make them again. You can look to the future with pride instead of being weighed down by shame over your past.

Take pride in having a disciplined routine. We're not suggesting that you instigate some around-the-clock military-style discipline but that you set yourself some simple rules. For instance, rules about what time you get up in the morning, how much television you watch, when you eat and what time you go to bed. Your previous life was robbed of all discipline by your addiction and suddenly reintroducing some sort of discipline is a good way to introduce structure and purpose to your new life.

Take pride in your appearance. Let's face it, you probably weren't at your best when you were high on drink or drugs. Start to show the world the new you. This doesn't mean Armani suits or designer frocks, just taking care of yourself and presenting a new image to the world. You can use this episode in your life positively and creatively and give your old life a radical new overhaul.

Q. What types of gambling cause problems?

A. Any and all forms of betting – from the dogs and horse racing to scratchcards and casino games. Online gambling is also becoming a growing problem for some.

Belonging not isolation

Start to feel part of the world again rather than feeling isolated at the margins. As an addict, you were living in your own private bubble either afraid or unwilling to let anybody in. You may have had drinking buddies or friends in the drug scene but, as your dependence grew, even this company became impossible to sustain. In the end, it was you and the bottle or you and the tablets, for example – and nobody else was allowed into your gradually shrinking world.

Begin to rediscover what it means to be part of a wider society. You could begin with the family. Enjoy interacting with your partner and children, for example, asking them about their day, or making plans for the weekend together. We said that shared meal times are important. So are the thousand and one other moments in the day when you can share the washing up, the school run, even something as simple as a joke or a story with the kids. The payback will be enormous. After having been cut off from family members for so long you'll find yourself welcomed back.

Q. How quickly can I become addicted to drugs?

A. This is a very difficult question with no easy answers. All drugs not specifically prescribed for a medical condition are dangerous, damaging and potentially lethal. The ease with which you can become addicted depends on your body chemistry and your mental state.

Consider linking up with a club or a society, joining a choir, helping out with the parent teacher association at school, joining your local community or church group, or doing voluntary work for one afternoon a week. These are all ways of participating in life rather than sitting back passively and letting it wash over you. These sorts of organizations can represent real lifelines at a time of great personal stress.

MYTH: Alcohol makes sex better and more exciting.

FACT: Alcohol lowers inhibitions and gives the impression of increased sexual desire but excessive drinking dulls physical sensation. Good sex is about understanding your partner's needs and desires and communicating your own.

Strength not fear

To get as far as you have, you must be strong. We're not talking about muscles and brawn here but determination, a desire to change, and a willingness to confront your demons – qualities that are at the root of real strength. So tell yourself you are strong.

Just as you can go to the gym, lift weights, and work out to develop your muscles, so you can do things that will develop your inner strength. Each time you say no to a drink, each time you resist the temptation to check the pools results or buy a scratchcard, you are putting yourself through a healthy emotional workout that will make you stronger. Each time you get on the front foot and square up to your fears you are growing in strength and confidence.

Every night before you go to bed, think of the progress you've made that day, and every morning when you wake, think of repeating the success of yesterday. That's how to develop real strength and it's just as effective as spending three hours on the rowing machine.

Nobody chooses to become an addict. It happens. Or more correctly, we allow it to happen. **Real strength lies in choosing to get well.**

Hope not depression

Every one of us, whether a recovering addict or not, will have days when we feel miserable for no apparent reason. That's to be expected. But to be low day after day, month in month out is not normal and, if you find yourself falling into that trap, it's time to do something about it.

All the things we've talked about already – from diet and exercise, to keeping busy and helping others – will contribute to your mental and physical well-being. But most of all it's hope in the future that will help keep you afloat. New possibilities *are* beginning to open up to you and you should focus on to the fact that, despite the odd low moment, your future is immeasurably brighter and more hopeful than your past.

There's a useful phrase you may have heard: 'Change what you can, accept what you can't.' By now you will be aware of all the changes you have already made. Now start to consider the changes that you think might be possible in the future: changes in domestic routines, changes in friendships, changes in priorities, and changes in personal outlook and expectation. Begin to look to a productive and optimistic future that both you and your family can enjoy.

There will be some things you cannot change, the most obvious being your future abstinence from drink, drugs or gambling. That is non-negotiable. You will have to be prepared to summon the effort of will day by day to accept that you will probably never touch a beer, a scotch or a glass of wine, for example, ever again. It will sound hard at first but, once you get used to the reality, it will be manageable. Change what you can, accept what you can't. That's where real hope lies. If you can hold on to that, you'll have the mental and emotional stamina to survive feeling low when the going gets tough.

In the past you probably reached for the bottle, the tablets, or the cards when life got too hard to bear. But did that do any good? Didn't it drive you further and further down the spiral of decline? Try the new option. Try reversing the direction of the destructive spiral and transforming it into something that's leading you upwards towards a bright and hopeful future.

Before we bring this section to a close, let us just say that we're not trying to tell you what you should or should not do. Were trying to make suggestions rather than lay down the law. You might find some of the suggestions helpful to your circumstances and some not. You can pick and choose. All of the issues mentioned here have been mentioned by recovering addicts themselves over the years. For some people, these have been very important in the whole process of recovery. We list them here to suggest the approaches you can make but we're not here to enforce them. Take from this book only the things you find helpful – you know best what will suit your own lifestyle and personality.

Rebuilding a life

Rebuilding a new life sometimes means demolishing the old one. There may be bits you can salvage from the old structure to incorporate into the new but, by and large, you're going to have to resign yourself to wiping the slate clean and starting again. Here's a true story for you.

As a result of a mid-life divorce, Jack had to trade down properties and find himself a modest house while his ex-wife lived in the marital home. Jack found a reasonable house in a not too smart area of south London and moved in. The property was within his price range because it was very old-fashioned and, crucially, boasted an eyesore of a conservatory that Jack used as the kitchen. Conservatory was too grand a word for this ramshackle construction that stood out like a sore thumb at the back of the house. Nobody else would have given the house a second glance but Jack, because of the need for economy, had snapped it up.

For four years, he put up with this rudimentary kitchen, apologizing to guests for the state of the place and steering visitors away from the wreck at the back of the house. One day he had had enough and lost his patience. He simply had to do something about the terrible kitchen. But what? He had very little money after all. He sat down and considered his options. There were two.

He could do nothing and carry on as before, putting up with the squalor and inconvenience of a kitchen that local authority inspectors would probably have condemned had they seen it. Or he could knock it down and rebuild something better. He went for option two. It wasn't an easy decision to make since he had to arrange a considerable bank loan. Yet he figured that the alternative was worse.

Before building work could start, he had to demolish the conservatory. It was tricky because, without it, he now had no kitchen at all. He resigned himself to the disruption, knowing that in six or eight months he would be moving into an extension that he could at last be proud of. It was immensely satisfying to say goodbye and good riddance to the old structure and, a few months later, to be sitting in a comfortable kitchen of which he no longer need be ashamed.

And here's an optimistic postscript. Before the extension was built, Jack's house (virtually unsaleable) was valued at £110,000. After the extension was completed at a cost of £40,000, the house was revalued at £250,000. He thought he couldn't afford the extension at first. What's clear is that he certainly couldn't have afforded not to!

Now, think of your addictive lifestyle as that clapped out conservatory that appalled visitors and made Jack wince. OK, it's hard to dismantle a lifestyle you've got used to (just as it was hard for Jack to finance the project in the first place). However, think of the gains you make when you replace a destructive lifestyle with something more wholesome.

Of course, change will come at a cost – in Jack's case the disruption of having no kitchen for six months, in yours the discomfort of going without the drink, drugs, or gambling you relied on. Yet look at the gains. From the very moment Jack set about demolishing that eyesore, he realized for the first time that something more impressive and better was possible. That's how it is with your life now. Your old ways will have to come crumbling down, reduced to a pile of rubble on the ground. In their place you can erect new patterns of life that will be ten times better than the old. Focus on that thought as you rebuild your new improved life and think of the profit *you* stand to make from a complete change of life.

Enjoying the new life

As Jack is now enjoying his comfortable new kitchen with all mod-cons and with sliding patio doors looking out onto the garden, you can begin to sit back and enjoy the view from where you are.

You've come a long way from the traumatic days when you first admitted you needed help, and you've done well to stay the course. We hope you will continue to persevere as we move on to Part 3, which looks at the strategies necessary for your long-term survival.

In the meantime, start to enjoy the new life you're making for yourself. It's full of surprising possibilities and it can change in the most delightful ways. True, there are great dangers out there as well as delights. Your new life won't stop you from getting ill, it won't protect you from bereavement, or disappointment or upset – nothing will – but it will give you the confidence to meet all these challenges as a responsible, functioning member of society. In the past, you may have run away from any challenges and sought refuge in drink, drugs, gambling or anything that would numb you to the pain of living. The trouble is you were also anaesthetizing yourself to life's pleasures. Start to feel. **Start to live again.**

Part 3:
Settling into
the Journey

It's time to take a breather. Whether you're the recovering addict or the partner or carer, you've certainly earned it. The immediate crisis has passed and you've applied the first aid. Now you can start to concentrate on the long-term road to recovery. We hope by now you're feeling calmer about the journey ahead, more able to contemplate the future in a measured sort of way without the old feelings of panic and desperation you had when you were at rock bottom. The fact is that the worst is probably behind you and, in the words of the old cliché, things can only get better. You should take real comfort from that.

8

Looking ahead

So what next? The simple answer is this: enjoy your new life. The past months have been marked by quite a lot of hardship, probably some tears and a lot of hard knocks. Well done for enduring them and coming through. Now it's time to experience the rewards that will surely come from all that hard work. True, there will be tough moments up ahead from time to time but that's only to be expected; life isn't all plain sailing. And life – the life that you were once insulated from by your drink, drugs or gambling – can be hard. The real challenge is to face life's realities head on rather than running away from them by seeking temporary comfort in illusions. Yes, there will be hardships and pains, but also joys and pleasures. Welcome back to real life with all its possibilities.

Hope

Hope is the first essential you should equip yourself with for the long term. You can change – you have changed – and you know now that the old life can be turned around for good. You know now that, however far you fell, you picked yourself up again and began to rebuild a good and productive life. You may even find yourself in a position to help others and to turn your negative experiences into positive ones – you have hope for the future.

Nonetheless, you should hold on to a tiny part of that past – both as a warning and as an encouragement. We're not suggesting that you live in the past or cling on to harmful elements of your previous life, but that you keep in mind an image of just how bad things were. Choose one snapshot of your old life. This might be the time when you ended up in the gutter, or that lost weekend spent high on painkillers, or that loss on the horses when you squandered a month's wages. Hold that image in your mind's eye and take a look at it from time to time. You'll probably do this with a shiver, realizing just how far you sank. Let it stand as a warning. Use it to underline the fact that you never ever want to be there again. However, that snapshot can also act as an encouragement to you – it is hope. Let it remind you that you've escaped the clutches of the bottle, the pills or the gambling and that you've successfully moved on.

MYTH: Compulsive gambling is a rich man's problem.

FACT: Problem gambling affects men and women from all walks of life. Gambling becomes a problem when it takes over from all other concerns in life. The actual amounts spent are a side issue although the results will be catastrophic on an individual's personal life and finances.

Strength

Another essential is strength, which you're beginning to realize by now comes in many forms. We're not talking about muscle power or of some superhuman ability to bear extremes of pain and suffering; it's more the quiet resolve to endure and accept what life throws at you without too much fuss or complaint. Realistically you'll have a lot to endure in terms of occasional stress, temptation and discomfort. No one knows that better than you. You will need to reach into your reserves of strength which come in the form of an attitude of mind. Say to yourself, 'I am strong. I must be because I've come this far. So I'm going to be strong again to weather this temporary rough patch.'

Routine

Many recovering addicts say that one of the most important things to develop in the long term is a routine. This will vary from person to person and need not be a rigid schedule that accounts for every waking moment. It just needs to be a broad framework that gives structure to your day. Getting up at a certain time, going for a walk, doing the household chores, going out for a weekend drive in the country, having a family lunch on Sunday, or going to bed at a set time in the evening are the most obvious examples of an easy routine that you could follow. Look at the pattern of your life and create a routine that suits your individual circumstances.

You may find it useful to have a small noteboard in the kitchen. Then you can plan your day or your week ahead and tick off the things you've done as you do them. Making lists – and having them on public display on the fridge or cupboard door – can be a real encouragement. What's more, it's a visible reminder that you have done all those things you said you would.

Activity

Closely linked to a routine (and just as helpful for the recovering addict) is activity. You'll find that you have more free time available now you've abandoned trips to the pub or the betting shop so it's essential that you **keep busy**.

We've already mentioned the variety of hobbies and leisure interests you could pursue. These are useful but they don't necessarily reflect everything we mean by 'being busy'. Like the kind of strength we described earlier, being busy is more an attitude of mind. This means having a purpose and a point to your life, having goals to achieve, setting yourself targets, and taking pleasure and satisfaction in seeing them met. In practice, this could be anything from deciding you are going to spend more quality time with your partner and children to buying a newspaper every day and reading it from cover to cover. If you live alone, you may want to focus on deepening friendships and arranging to meet regularly every month, for example. It's all a question of doing something – often anything – in preference to sitting around thinking.

Faith

Have faith. By this, we don't necessarily mean faith in God or in an almighty creator of the universe. Have faith in people and in yourself. Have faith that the world can be made better and that you can personally, in all sorts of small ways, leave it in a better state than that which you found it. Believe that you can make a difference to things. You've already begun to make a difference to your own life and to change your destructive ways into something positive, so start to believe that you can make a difference to the bigger picture. You've come through a crisis and survived. Now turn the crisis into an opportunity – an opportunity to enjoy a new life to the full.

Patience

Patience is another quality worth developing. You may not find this easy at first – after all, you've been used to the instant gratification of alcohol or pills or the immediate excitement of a trip to the casino. You probably want everything now, including your recovery. Nonetheless, settling into this new life of yours is a gradual procedure that will be achieved by small steps not giant leaps. Be patient. It's a cumulative process; over time, all the small things you do will add up to real change.

Think of yourself driving a car, gradually approaching a fork in the road. All it takes is a tiny turn of the wheel left or right to take you in an entirely different direction. That small movement will determine the course of your journey utterly and completely. Similarly the small alterations you make in your routine and in your outlook will dictate your own personal route to recovery.

Don't try to overreach yourself by setting yourself ambitious challenges and impossible goals. Make the small changes and aim for the achievable targets and you will find yourself surprised and delighted by the progress you've made. For example, every year groups of youngsters volunteer to help out in the UK's ancient cathedrals, doing some of the million and one chores needed to maintain the fabric of these beautiful buildings. One group had been assigned the job of cleaning the small tiles that made up an enormous pavement in one of the side chapels. The young lad buffing up the tiles with a duster and a tub of polish said at first that the job seemed pointless and boring. All he ever got to look at was one tile at a time and polishing a 15-cm (6-inch) square surface seemed to be making not the slightest bit of difference. He seemed to be getting nowhere and felt like packing it all in. But then, after a couple of hours, he stopped and looked back behind him to see what he *had* achieved. He saw hundreds of tiles, each one painstakingly polished and cleaned of centuries of grime, gleaming in the sunlight. The effect, he said, was magical and made all his hard work worthwhile. So it will be for you. **Be patient and you'll get there.** Don't be afraid to be the tortoise rather than the hare.

Moving forward

One of the first things to realize as a recovering addict is that you now have a future. In the old days, the future extended as far as the next drink, the next hit, or the next trip to the betting shop. Beyond that was another drink, another hit, another trip to and so on. Now you can plan a life beyond those miserable confines and begin to look ahead.

This can be a little daunting at first. Will you be able to stay sober for good? Will you be able to maintain a drug-free lifestyle for months and years ahead? Will you be able to live without the buzz and the shared camaraderie of the betting office for what will be, realistically, the rest of your life? These are the wrong questions to ask yourself. The real questions are:

- Do I really want to go back to the old life of drug, alcohol or gambling dependency when I've managed to climb out of that dark pit of addiction?

- Do I really want to put this whole journey of recovery into reverse now that I've come this far?

- Do I really want to jeopardize the present and the future to return to my destructive past?

When you turn the question around to focus on your real priorities, you'll find that the future need not hold fears and worries. It can be a future made up of lasting promise and limitless possibilities. Start to ask the positive questions instead of the negative ones. Replace 'How can I go without a drink for the rest of my life?' with 'What are the new things I can do if I stay sober?'

MYTH: Drinkers are often the life and soul of the party and there's nothing more boring than an ex-alcoholic who's given up.

FACT: Heavy drinkers who regularly get drunk can become extremely tiresome. You don't need drink to have an interesting evening. Recovering alcoholics won't insist you don't drink, but they're content not to do so themselves. It isn't boring to stop wanting to drink yourself to death.

Recovery

If you've undergone a professionally supervised programme of detoxification, your physical recovery should have begun 10 to 15 days after you first entered it. There are certain exceptions, such as those with severe liver damage or brain impairment or those suffering benzodiazepine withdrawal, that can take a few weeks longer. However, ultimate recovery takes far longer than a fortnight or three weeks, and you'll need to get yourself mentally prepared for this lengthier timescale.

You will feel noticeably better and more positive after the initial treatment, but the danger is that you'll feel 'cured' when you are anything but. After the initial high comes a depressing dip when you contemplate an endless future without the physical, mental, and emotional crutches of the bottle or the pills. Try to shift your perpective by not viewing the future as an infinity of 'doing without' something but beginning to see it as a fulfilling time when you'll be able to *do* all sorts of new things.

Recovery involves changing your behaviour. It's not an easy thing for most of us to do because we love our comfort zones too much and easily get set in our ways. As a result, most of us change only when we have to – often after a traumatic or negative event like a bereavement, a serious road accident, a divorce, redundancy or illness. There's no doubt about the effort you, as a recovering addict, will need to expend in your bid for wholeness and well-being. Remember that mental snapshot you chose as both a warning and an encouragement in Chapter 7? Well, as you look ahead to the future in a positive way, occasionally take time to look at the negative implications of not continuing your new life of sobriety. We have talked a lot about carrots so far. Time for a few words about sticks.

Ask yourself what would happen to your domestic life, your working life, and your personal life if you relapsed into alcoholism, drug abuse or reckless gambling. You already know the answer. Your relationships with your partner, children, and friends would deteriorate and crumble into ruins; you would be faced with the prospect of unemployment, financial ruin, and loss of any professional standing in the world; and your own life would lose all purpose and promise. In short, you would have thrown your life away.

You have a responsibility to your family and your friends not to let this happen again. It may sound harsh but we are talking about serious, grown-up issues. To repeat, we are talking about potentially throwing your whole life away. It's that serious. If you are the sole breadwinner in the family you have a duty to keep your dependants protected and secure, both financially and emotionally.

The Hollywood film *Awakenings* (1990), starring Robert de Niro and Robin Williams, is based on a true story centring on a group of patients who suffered from a mysterious epidemic of sleeping sickness affecting a number of people in the 1950s and 1960s. Those unfortunate enough to contract the disease fell into a coma that lasted years, often decades. Cruelly, all the while they were conscious of their immobility and their helplessness. It was like a kind of death, but one where they knew they were alive yet incapable of functioning normally.

In real life, neurosurgeon Dr Sacks discovered that by administering a particular drug in controlled quantities his patients could be brought out of their coma and, as it were, brought back to life. The results were truly astonishing and film exists of some of the men and women who had fallen into a coma aged 20 being revived 40 years later. We see 60-year-olds singing the songs and dancing the dances that they learned four decades ago as if they had been suspended in time and had resumed their lives at the point at which their lives had been cut off.

Sadly, the final outcome did not live up to its initial promise and it became clear that higher and higher doses of the drug were needed to produce less and less of an effect. The elderly people were becoming weaker and weaker and, one by one, relapsing into the coma they had known and feared for most of their lives. In the film, the worst affected is Leonard (played by Robert de Niro) who, in that all too brief period of 'awakening', forms an attachment with a young woman and has a tantalizing glimpse of what it could be like to live a full life once again.

Leonard is an intelligent man and knows exactly what is going on. In his conversations with Dr Sacks he makes it clear that he knows full well that the drug is not working and that he, too, is slowly relapsing into a coma-like state, probably for the remainder of his life. In one heartbreaking outburst in the film, he accuses Dr Sacks of treating him like a guinea pig, of bringing him back to life only to have to condemn him to 'death' once again. Just at the point when he has awoken to life's possibilities, Leonard is cruelly denied the chance to enjoy them and he feels 'like Lazarus made to do his dying all over again.'

This is a truly heart-rending predicament and we mention it at length as a warning and an encouragement. Leonard had no choice in the matter. You have. Do you want to return to a state that could at times have been described as a living death? Or do you want to choose life – the new life you have begun to enjoy and the life that would be tantalizingly taken from you if you fell back into the old ways?

MYTH: If you put enough money into a slot machine you will eventually win.

FACT: Machines are programmed over time to pay out less than is put in.

Planning the future

Sober, clean, and free of the corrosive compulsion to gamble your money and your life away, you have a life of promise to look forward to. You can start to plan and to dream again. You can work on long-term projects and schemes from spending time with the family to helping others through charity work or from building your own house to retiring to the country. The fact is that you have a clean slate on which to write anything you choose.

Learn to enjoy the freedom and the peace of mind that brings. It won't immunize you against life's hard knocks but with a renewed outlook you'll be better placed to cope with those hard knocks and, crucially, to enjoy all that life has to offer.

We've talked about the value of lists and writing them up on your noteboard in the kitchen. What we suggest now is a similar thing but on a larger scale. Start drawing up a bigger life plan with long-term goals that you can work on over time. Don't worry if you don't achieve all of these; the point is that you look further into the future than you have up to now.

So far you have followed the one-step-at-a-time approach, concentrating on getting by from week to week, day to day and, right at the start, from hour to hour. Now, we hope you're starting to enjoy the possibility of planning months and maybe years ahead while believing, with a high degree of confidence, that you're still going to be addiction-free by the time those deadlines come around. Start to enjoy the planning stage and experience the thrill of anticipation. This can be just as satisfying on your own or with a friend as it is with your partner.

Finances willing, try to take holidays, bargain breaks, or special deal weekends. It doesn't have to cost a fortune and you don't have to take a holiday every other week. These can be the special treats that keep your mind on the fact that you now have a present and a future to enjoy. You may also like to think about a complete change of holiday venue. Holidays are often food and drink oriented – possibly with a casino experience thrown in. Temptations like that, quite obviously, should be avoided. So what's the alternative?

You could consider something new – an activity holiday of some sort. You may fancy white-water rafting or mountaineering but, if not, choose one of the less challenging alternatives. There are hundreds of companies specializing in walking holidays. Give it a go. Holidays can cater for singles, couples, families and for groups – taking you on easy walks through the loveliest parts of the countryside. The beauty of these holidays is that you're always active, walking and talking one minute and gazing at the scenery the next. The landscape constantly changes, you keep yourself fit, and you're not spending much money. Not only that, you finish the day pleasantly tired and ready for an early night – instead of contemplating a night on the town with all the traps that entails. If walking's not for you think about cycling. Again there are many companies offering leisurely cycling tours, providing all the equipment, and planning interesting routes for you. All you have to do is pedal.

If you want to take a bit more control, you could always plan a walking tour yourself. The excitement of anticipation coupled with the deep satisfaction of making a plan for the future – and sticking to it – are the real rewards of your new-found sobriety. You may raise a few eyebrows among your friends. Walking across England from coast to coast. Tramping the Pembrokeshire coastal path in the pouring rain. Camping on the Isle of Wight. Cycling through the Loire Valley. 'They've never done that before,' people will say, 'what's got into them?'

You may think this is beginning to read more like a holiday brochure than a book on addiction, but all of these things are practical suggestions that you may find it useful to consider. It's all about breaking the mould of your old life in the simplest of ways and starting again. With a little thought on your part, you can easily come up with hundreds more ideas. Try to appreciate the infinity of possibilities that are now open to you; it takes only small changes in behaviour and attitude to alter the entire course of your life.

9

Hard times and temptation

We're not going to lead you to believe that everything is going to be rosy all the time. Some will find change easier than others and may find that a life of activity and walking holidays really does do the trick. Others will find abstinence a real trial, both a physical and mental hurdle that they have to face every day of their lives.

> *MYTH: I wouldn't be 'me' if I gave up drink, drugs or gambling.*
>
> **FACT:** You are always 'you'. It depends which 'you' you choose: the person who's destroying himself or the person who's leading a productive life.

There are no easy answers to abstinence. For some it will be a constant battle and no amount of talking and explaining will take away the sheer discomfort of refraining from drink, drugs or gambling. We can only say, **have faith and keep strong**. The battle can be won and millions of ordinary men and women have made heroic efforts to win it. They labour day by day in the face of enormous temptation – and day by day they get through. It can be done, albeit at an enormous cost in discipline and personal resolve. Take heart from the millions worldwide who are just like you and who are winning their personal battles hour by hour and day by day.

That said, there are practical ways in which you can weather the hard times and avoid temptations. One of these is to identify the so-called triggers that prompt a possible relapse.

Environmental triggers

Environmental triggers can be physical locations or occasions which can, in the case of alcoholism, trigger a return to the old patterns of drinking. For example:

- Bars and pubs

- Social clubs

- Golf clubs and the 19th hole

- Christmas and New Year celebrations

- Book or product launches

- Awards ceremonies

- Opening nights

- Gala evenings

- Wedding receptions

- Anniversary celebrations

- Socializing after work.

For ex-gamblers environment triggers will include:

- Casinos

- Betting shops

- The sport results pages of local and national newspapers

- Lottery results programmes

- Slot machine arcades.

For illegal drug abusers environment triggers will include:

- Night clubs

- Discos

- Raves

- Most peer group parties.

For prescription drug abusers environment triggers could include:

- Surgeries that collude in your prescription drug abuse

- The internet.

Are we suggesting that you never attend a wedding reception ever again, that you never go to the opening night of a movie or an art exhibition? Are we suggesting that you never socialize with friends after work or never attend a Christmas party or go to the golf club? No.

We are suggesting that you realize that certain locations and certain experiences under certain circumstances at certain times may not be healthy for you. You will want to go out after work with a couple of mates, but you need to ask yourself whether you are strong enough to resist 'a quick one' or 'just the one'. If you feel you aren't, say 'no'. Your real friends will understand and you can always go out with them again on another occasion when you're feeling strong enough to get by on a lime juice and soda.

If you're feeling vulnerable at Christmas or New Year, try to make alternative arrangements. Arrange a party at home where you can control the drinks – alcoholic or otherwise – and enjoy the festivities on your terms.

Learn to avoid the occasions when you might be faced with temptation. It's not a snub to your artist friend to turn down the invitation to his or her private view just because you know there'll be wine sloshing around. Explain to them why you'd prefer not to come on the first night, but make it clear that you'll be turning up at the gallery the following week when all the razzmatazz has died down.

It's up to you to decide what you can and can't get through. Be aware that on some of the occasions listed above there'll be extra pressure and extra temptation. **Learn to spot the warning signs** and the triggers and take appropriate evasive action.

Stress and worry

Life, as they say, is best defined as one thing after another. Life is stress, life is worry – plus lots of other things besides. However, in your condition, excessive stress and worry are potentially hazardous. How do you protect yourself against them? The simple answer is: you can't. But we're asking the wrong question. The right question is: how should you best proceed when you are stressed or worried?

First, you need to practise self-awareness. Develop the antennae that warn you that pressures are building up at home or at work and realize that you need to manage them.

If you've fallen out with your partner and had some petty row that's got out of all proportion, make the effort to extend an olive branch. Meet them halfway. Not only will this do wonders for your relationship, it will also bring your stress levels right down.

If the children are giving you a hard time, try to have a calm word with them, explaining why you think their behaviour is unacceptable. A family is a community and a society in miniature, and to function properly there needs to be a little give and take. Of course, it's not always so simple dealing with teenagers who always know best, but attempting some sort of dialogue may go halfway to providing a solution.

If work is going badly, talk it over with business partners, life partners, friends and trusted colleagues, possibly even with your boss. If you feel you're being passed over or that you're being treated unfairly and are in line for that raft of compulsory redundancies, find yourself a person you can open up to.

The reality is that talking about the stress won't necessarily stop it. Being open and honest about your fears over redundancy, for example, won't necessarily stop you getting fired but it will help you to deal with the situation as it arises. It will reduce the stress and the fear surrounding it. There is a simple choice: would you prefer redundancy, or redundancy with a return to alcoholism?

Recognize that if you allow yourself to get stressed or worried, you are putting your recovery at risk. Worries can become the trigger that prompt a relapse, and you need to be constantly on the look out for the danger signals.

At times of stress, time for yourself and relaxation becomes important. Get enough fresh air and exercise. Take long walks in the park or into town. Go to bed early, eat healthily, take a long soak in a hot bath, listen to your favourite music, practise relaxation techniques (see Part 5, page 287), do a large and complicated jigsaw – anything to help you wind down. It won't take the problem away but it will clear your head and help you to deal with it more effectively and, crucially for you, this will lessen the chance of your weakening.

Lack of motivation

This is a common complaint when people are some way into recovery but not quite there. The excitement of the first few weeks' life changes has passed, the thrill of the new lifestyle has died down, and the initial optimism surrounding your major resolution has faded a little. So what now? Is that all there is?

Anticlimaxes are to be expected. They happen to everybody. Don't be surprised and dismayed by them; be prepared for them and have a strategy in place to deal with them. Your first port of call is the cognitive therapy option (see page 71).

Regardless of how you feel – indeed, in flat contradiction to what your emotions are telling you – remind yourself what you've achieved. Let your reason and your head tell you how far you've come and that you still have further to go. Get out the lists, the diaries, the journals and the schedules – all the things you've written down and successfully done and hold them up as visible proof of your continuing progress, however demotivated you may feel.

Now do something. Anything. Rather than sit there feeling like a a limp lettuce. Go for a swim, do the ironing, wash the car, clean the bathroom, go to the shops, make a cuppa, bake a cake, exercise the dog, mow the lawn, rearrange your CD collection, go for a drive – *do* something. First you will find that you're engrossed in something purely mechanical, which is taking your mind off things. Second, you realize the blank moment has passed and miraculously been replaced by a lighter mood.

Telling yourself that your recovery isn't working, that it's taking too long, or that you've lost all interest in recovery at all is the alarm bell warning you that you are potentially at your most vulnerable. Doing something is a way of buying yourself some time to let that scary moment pass. Merely sitting there and thinking the same old negative thoughts over and over in your head could make you more likely to relapse. Spot the triggers in advance and be ready for them.

Myth: Drinking and drug-taking make me more imaginative and creative.

Fact: Drinking and drug-taking make you think you are more creative. Heavy drinking and drug-taking are incompatible with the sustained effort that goes into any creative endeavour.

10

Looking back

Up until now, you've had your eye either on the next step you're taking or on the road ahead. You can now take a look behind you and spend a little time reflecting on how you came to be here in the first place. If you're following an Alcoholics or Gamblers Anonymous programme or if you're having drug counselling, the likelihood is that you are already looking at the underlying causes of your addictive behaviour. This chapter is a way of reinforcing that therapy and allowing you to come to terms with some of the factors that may have led you into a particular form of destructive behaviour.

Typically, the way you are experiencing your recovery will be the opposite of the way in which your alcoholism or your drug-taking first took hold. The first stage of recovery involved the physical withdrawal of the drink, drugs or gambling and moved towards the emotional and the mental treatment of the condition. By contrast, the disease started with an underlying emotional or mental dysfunction that gradually manifested itself as a physical dependence.

Factors of addiction

As part of your long-term recovery, it's now worth thinking about some of the initial factors that may have led you into substance abuse or gambling. If you can put your finger on what was troubling you or making your life seem incomplete or unsatisfactory *without* drink drugs or gambling you may be in a better position to understand how you got into this mess and how you can stay out of it.

Realistically, many people do not go in for this kind of analysis. It may not be your style. That's fine. However, if you find it does help to review your life to try to come to terms with it better, the following (far from exhaustive) lists may provide some sort of road map.

Taking refuge in drink, drugs or gambling is often a way of avoiding difficult or painful experiences such as:

- Emotional and physical pain

- Family dysfunction

- Crises in life

- Boredom

- Trauma

- Unpleasant memories

- Depression

- Psychological distress

- Feelings of worthlessness

- Loneliness and isolation

- Damaged relationships.

> *MYTH: Drugs are just a phase every teenager goes through these days.*
>
> **FACT:** Most youngsters don't use drugs even though they're aware drugs are available. If they feel they can talk openly with parents and adults about what's on their mind, they're less likely to experiment.

At this stage in your recovery, ask yourself whether you recognize any of the above as triggers for your addiction. Perhaps there are elements of your personality that have led you into addiction and dependence. Look at the following list and tick any that you feel apply to you:

❏ An inability to communicate with others.

❏ Acute shyness that has made you retreat into a world of your own.

❏ Tension in your relationships with others – especially parents.

❏ Chronic frustration and a sense of never achieving anything.

❏ Feelings of guilt or inferiority.

❏ Intense competitiveness or perfectionism.

❏ Constant lack of self-esteem.

Now you might like to look at some of the negative influences on your life and at people and circumstances that may have contributed to your addictive and destructive way of life:

- Parents who constantly rowed

- Parents who had consistently low expectations of you

- Parents who had consistently high expectations and who expressed annoyance or anger when you failed to live up to them

- A father who openly despised or mistreated your mother (or vice versa)

- An incidence or incidences of sexual abuse – especially by a relative or trusted friend of the family

- Physical or chronic verbal abuse

- Lack of demonstrative physical contact as a child

- Chronic lack of affection

- Lack of family discipline and parental boundaries

- Parents who regularly left you on your own

- A mother or father who was clearly unhappy with his or her lot as a parent

- A family environment in which problems and issues were swept under the carpet rather than discussed in the open

- A family history of alcoholism or drug abuse.

These are far from being exhaustive lists of the factors that may have contributed to your former condition, but they may be guides. At this point, it's important to issue a warning. It's about your measure of personal responsibility.

Many people have parents who constantly rowed but never themselves became alcoholics. Many people have families who find it hard to communicate or who have unreasonable expectations of their children and they don't become dependent on drink or drugs. In themselves, the things listed above need not necessarily lead to substance dependence or gambling. There will always be another element, often very difficult to pin down, that tips one person into addiction and leaves another untouched.

In the quiet of your own thoughts or in the hands of a skilled counsellor or even in late night conversations with a partner or a trusted friend, you may be able to work towards and identify some of the reasons that led you to where you are. Identifying and naming some factors that had a negative influence on you may help to understand where you've come from and to work out how you proceed from here.

You must also accept your share of responsibility, as an adult, for your former condition. Many men and women have undergone appalling physical neglect and horrifying sexual and emotional abuse and they don't become addicts. It is not enough to apportion blame without at least taking some personal responsibility. This separates grown-up behaviour from childish, dependent, or immature behaviour. Avoid, if you can, the sort of mentality that casts you constantly in the role of victim. Don't be a victim of someone else's behaviour anymore; be an adult who chooses to take full responsibility for his or her actions. This is real strength and real character, and in the long run, this could turn out to be the single most important factor in your recovery.

11

Enjoying the moment

After the soul-searching of Chapter 10, let's turn our attention from the past to the here and now. You need to develop a full appreciation of the present. This is the best guarantee of recovery, and once you achieve it you'll be far less likely to slip into your old world of illusion, short-term gratification, and long-term despair.

Survival strategies

There is no single way of achieving a full appreciation of the present but we can suggest a few survival strategies. In the end, it will be for you and your loved ones to find out what works for you. All our lives are different, all our circumstances are varied, and our personalities are many. However, there is one overarching approach that unites us all: ultimate recovery from addiction flows in some way or other from restored and healthy human relationships.

You can't recover on your own. Indeed you can't enjoy life on your own – whether you've been an addict or not. At some profound and basic level, humans are social creatures who need company and human contact to survive and flourish. This is why the drink and the drugs were so corrosive. They cut you off from others, isolating you in your own bubble of illusion and contentment. Ex- gamblers often say they enjoyed the sense of shared camaraderie in the betting office among like-minded people. But was that a real relationship with any substance outside the betting shop or the casino? Did you have anything else in common other than this obsessive and headlong plunge into momentary excitement? Would you have spent time with each other talking about your families, your hopes or your goals and ambitions? Probably not. The camaraderie of like-minded addicts is not the stuff of real friendship; like the mood induced by drink and drugs, it's illusory and short lived.

Start to develop relationships that will last and bear fruit. Begin with your partner who has seen you at your worst, stuck with you (just), and who has had to bear the brunt of your unreasonable and, let's face it, often outrageous behaviour. They've really suffered. Perhaps not in obvious ways or in the visible way that you have, but they've suffered. If their distress wasn't visible, it may have been because you were too drunk, driven or out of it to notice.

Try to make amends and say you're sorry, but don't leave it there. Don't wallow in self-pity and tearful expressions of regret because the chances are your partner has had enough of tears – their own! The best expression of regret is the desire and the promise to change, to draw a line under the past and to resolve to live sober or clean in the present and the future.

Sadly, some marriages and relationships won't survive the stress. If one party, after due and deliberate consideration, decides to leave a marriage, no power on earth will persuade them to return. People divorce not because they want to but because they have to. Even in this worst-case scenario there is always hope. The hope, for the ex-addict, is that change is possible. With heroic effort and self-denial, with painful self-knowledge and long-term resolve, the recovering alcoholic, drug abuser or gambler can move on. It may be a very different life from the one you used to lead, but it can be fulfilling. It may be without the partner you loved and pushed away or who could take no more, but a changed and productive life is possible.

If you have a family, rediscover your children. Rediscover the nobility of responsible mother- or fatherhood. If your children are young, they'll easily bounce back. They'll be so delighted to have the mother or father they once knew returned to them that they'll carry you along in their sheer joy and enthusiasm. Put them, not yourself, at the centre of your life and you'll find that miraculously it's you who will benefit just as much. You'll discover the truth of the phrase: better to give than receive.

If your children are older and have suffered years of neglect or unreasonable behaviour on your part, if they've felt guilty or ashamed that their father or mother was not like a 'normal' mum or dad, then you're certainly going to have to work harder. However, if you can open a dialogue with them, start to talk to them openly and honestly, and show them by your actions that you want to change, it is possible to repair damaged relationships. Even if your children are grown up themselves with children of their own, it's never too late to start the process of repair.

If you can't summon the courage to speak to your children face to face after so long spent burying real emotions beneath the surface, think about writing a letter. This doesn't have to be a literary work it doesn't even have to be long. Write a sincere and honest account of how you're feeling and how you'd like to rebuild the relationship. Give yourself a little space, take yourself to a quiet part of the house where you'll be on your own and undisturbed, and the words will come. You'll be amazed.

If you live alone, try to increase your circle of acquaintances. Try to develop a sense of community with people in your block, your street, your village or your town. Part 1 mentioned such things as joining choirs and evening classes or doing charity work at the school, church or community centre. At that point in your journey, those things helped to get you out of your rut and into activities that would take up your new-found free time. You may have tried one or two of them and found that they weren't for you, and some of the pursuits have fallen by the wayside.

At this point in your journey, such activities can have another and deeper purpose. Whether in the choir or at the charity shop, it's the people and the relationships that are important. The choir and the evening class may not be your cup of tea. No matter. Find something that is. It may be just chatting to your next-door neighbours and hearing about their lives and their views, but in that human interaction you can really find a sense of lasting purpose. For the recovering addict, rediscovering a sense of purpose is vital.

Reconnect with the physical world. One of the many things drink, drugs or gambling will have done is dull your senses. Start to enjoy them once again. Make the little things in life moments of celebration. Make a pot of fresh coffee and concentrate on the sensations of the moment, on its smell and its taste. Do the same with your tonic waters, herbal teas, juices and fizzy waters. Try to enjoy them as often as you can with others so that the talk and the company give you the buzz that alcohol, drugs or gambling once did.

This chapter is called 'Enjoying the moment', and that's the key to a real enjoyment of life. It's not always easy to achieve but it is something you can work towards in the simplest of ways. Imagine you're in a traffic jam quietly fuming that you're going nowhere. In the old days, that would be one of the stress triggers sending you to the bottle or the pills as soon as you arrived home. In your new recovering state, no such outlet is possible so learn to manage the stress. Say to yourself (cognitively), 'I'm stuck in a jam and there's nothing I can do about it. So I'll switch on the radio and just sit it out. If I'm late, I'm late. I'll change what I can and accept what I can't. I'll either bale out, park up, and take a bus or, if I can't, sit tight and enjoy the music.' Not easy, I know, but start to practise.

Although drink and drugs will have dulled your senses, the paradox is that you were almost certainly searching for a sensory experience when you drank or swallowed pills. You may have been trying to blot out all sense of feeling and to numb yourself to painful realities, but equally you may have been searching for that high, that buzz, that thrilling excitement that you felt everyday life could not offer. Yet everyday life is full of sensory experiences – from the look of happiness on a child's face to a brilliant sunset, from the smell of cut grass to the sound of waves crashing on the shore. Get up before dawn and watch the sun rise, go for a walk in the rain, take a jog through the woods and feel the springy pine needles beneath your feet. Enjoy the moment drug- and alcoho-free and you will discover the world as you've never experienced it before. We may be coming across a little strong, but it's fair to say your personality is one that has been drawn to extremes and intensity. The extremes you chose were harmful and damaging both to you and those around you, so choose intense experiences that occur naturally, with no downside and at no cost. Start to enjoy *real* life in all its intensity. There's no end to it. Get out there and find it, and when you've found it, **enjoy the moment**.

12

Long-term challenges

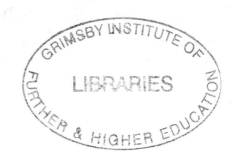

Long-term changes

Your principal challenge, of course, is staying drug- or alcohol-free and free of the compulsion to risk everything you own on the throw of the dice or the speed of a greyhound. The most important word here is '**free**'. The challenge is whether you have the strength of character to face up to all that freedom implies. Freedom is a scary thing and a surprising number of people, if they stopped to think about it, would realize that they are anything but free.

Freedom

How many people are trapped in a job, trapped in a damaging relationship, trapped in a repetitive compulsion to buy, shop and spend, or trapped in an endless cycle of television, soaps, game shows and football? How many would really exercise the freedom to break out of their comfort zone and do the things they say they would like to – become a mature student, train to be a nurse, travel the world, start up a business? How many are trapped by circumstances that prevent them from achieving their dreams?

However, this book is not for those people – it's for you in your own particular circumstances. What are you going to do to make the most of your new-found freedom? That's your challenge.

MYTH: Drink is what oils every social occasion.

FACT: Drink is all pervasive but it's the company that matters at any party not the alcohol.

Fear of change

If freedom is an important word for you right now so, too, is change. Change is never easy for anyone. In fact, it's so hard that most of us don't change unless we have to. Your long-term challenge is to confront your perfectly normal and understandable fear of change. You may be thinking that you don't have the willpower to stay sober for the rest of your life, that you don't have the mental stamina to keep out of the casino or the slot machine arcade, in short that you just can't hack this changed life of yours. Moreover, you may say to yourself that a life without a drink, a hit or the buzz of a big win on the horses isn't much of a life. You 'enjoyed' those sensations so much that you can't imagine a world without them. The following story may alter this persective.

The Jewish violinist Yitzhak Perlman, contracted polio as a boy and, as a result, walks with crutches and callipers on his legs. Contracting polio is nothing if not a major life change, but Perlman has weathered that change and, smiling broadly whenever he appears in public, produces the most sublime music any human being could produce. One evening

Perlman was performing a violin concerto and took his seat, as usual, centre stage. Twenty minutes in, there was an enormous crack that ricocheted around the hall like a bullet. A string on his violin had snapped. The audience froze for a split second but this virtuoso musician, without missing a beat, continued to play on three strings, altering his fingerwork to suit the new circumstances he was facing.

At the end of the performance, the audience rose to their feet and gave this genius a thundering ovation. Afterwards, Perlman was asked why he hadn't stopped the performance and arranged for a new string to be fitted. His reply, with heroic resignation and without a trace of self-pity was, 'We have to make music with what remains.'

Making music with what remains is your task. Your world has changed for good. It has also changed for the better – although it may not always feel that way when you are invaded by a sudden craving. You must now manage that change and find all that is positive, fulfilling and productive within it.

Twelve steps

If you've followed the 12-step programme of Alcoholics Anonymous or similar organizations, you will be familiar with their suggested pathway towards recovery. It's a tried and tested – and by common consent successful – programme of healing pioneered by men and women like yourself, compassionate human beings whose only concern is others' well-being.

If you haven't formally followed the programme, the challenge you face in the future lies in taking some or all of those 12 steps yourself and being aware of what they imply for the rest of your life. The first step is the admission that you were powerless over alcohol (or drugs or gambling) and that your life had become unmanageable as a result. Merely admitting this is a way of coping with the reality of your situation.

It follows that, if you are powerless, you will need some help from outside. Close family and friends will help but so, too, will the encouragement from people who have been in similar situations to your own. Recovering alcoholics and drug abusers who have been dry or clean for a year and more or who have experience of living without the crutch of gambling for a significant amount of time can explain the temptations you may encounter and the strategies for survival you can draw upon. They will be a constant encouragement to you to meet your challenges head on. Then, in time, you can pass on your advice and your experience to fellow sufferers. Taking and giving advice has the further benefit of restoring your sense of community, of reconnecting with people rather than living in isolation.

Steps two and three refer to a 'higher power' – or something akin to inner resources. The reasoning behind the 'higher power', is that sometimes when we admit we can't do something ourselves and humbly ask for help from others, things happen in ways we could never have imagined they would. Remember when we suggested that you write a letter to estranged family members in Chapter 11? We said that if you sit quietly for a moment the words will come. That's partly what is meant by a 'higher power', that something comes from a place buried so deep that you didn't know you had it until it appears, and it seems to appear in a way that's completely out of your control. It's the same with your recovery. Once you start to join forces with others, to talk and to share, a strength you never thought you had will emerge. Qualities you didn't know you possessed will come to the fore almost as if a 'higher power' were in control. It doesn't matter how you explain those qualities and that strength, what matters is that you discover them.

Step four involves a deep examination of yourself and an admission of your flaws and failings. This can be difficult and painful, but it's a useful way of making sense of your life before, during and after addiction. It involves writing down details about the relationships you've ruined, the people you've let down, the hurt you've caused and the promises you've broken. Step five is when you admit to yourself and others the nature of your mistakes.

Steps six and seven involve a promise to change and an appeal to the 'higher power' to help you. Steps eight, nine and ten ask you to make a list of the people you've hurt and to promise to make amends to them. This is not an easy task, but its purpose is to encourage you to face up to the personal damage your addiction has caused others and to help you, in so far as you can, to wipe the slate clean and start again with a new life.

Steps 11 and 12 have the theme of a 'spiritual awakening', enabling you to share your experiences with other people. Many people will be uneasy about the idea of a 'spiritual awakening'. This as an attempt to let you realize that you have undergone a profound and in some ways mysterious experience. Whatever you understand by the word 'spiritual', your life change and your new sense of purpose really do represent an awakening at a deep level. In your addictive state, it's as if you were in a deep sleep unaware of the world around you; now you've woken up to the world's possibilities and you're in a position to grow and develop as a responsible individual – an individual who's alert and responsive, not slumbering and dead to the world.

Awake, alert and vigilant

You face a constant challenge to realize that you are awake and alert to the world, alert to all the good things it has to offer and that you're willing and able to share them with others. When you start to connect with others, you start to belong to the rest of humanity (which for so long you had cut yourself off from). In doing so, you can develop strengths you never thought you had.

We're not talking about magic or some sort of hocus-pocus but other ex-addicts have said that they have experienced strange and unexpected transformations when they put their minds to recovery and developing a sense of communion with their fellow human beings.

Another challenge is to keep constantly vigilant. It's easy to coast or to let things slide and realistically most of us do that all the time. As an ex-addict aware of the traps and the temptations, you can't afford to do that. You, more than anyone, know what you stand to lose if you go back to a destructive way of life. Hard as it may sometimes be to keep sober or drug-free you know deep down that the alternative is far worse. Keep on your toes. Be aware of the triggers that could prompt a relapse and have strategies and coping mechanisms in place to deal with them. Know who your friends are and know that they're there for you in times of need.

As another part of vigilance, take care of yourself. Be kind to yourself and recognize that you have needs as well. You should be eating well, taking exercise and generally following the 'personal maintainance' routine we outlined in Part 1. That deals with the physical side of things but there's an emotional component to your life as well don't forget. Consider doing an emotional audit on yourself. From time to time, ask yourself some of the following questions:

- Am I generally feeling comfortable in my own skin?

- Am I feeling confident and secure in my working life?

- Am I feeling happy in my home life?

- Am I coping well with life's stresses and strains?

- Do I feel in control of my life?

- Do I feel connected to and valued by my family?

- Do I feel connected to the wider community?

- Am I broadly content with my status in life?

- Do I feel I'm generally valued outside the family?

This is not an exhaustive list, but it gives you an idea of some questions you can ask yourself about your general state of emotional well-being. We've talked about the value of helping others, but you too can hold a reasonable expectation of being helped and cared for. If you find yourself answering 'no' to a number of these questions, try talking things over with a close friend or sharing your unease with a partner. Communication is the key to solving many of life's difficulties.

Finally, remember that you are a special person with a special outlook on life. You have sunk to depths that most people will never imagine and undergone experiences most will never know. Yet, in daring to get well you have displayed strength and courage that the majority of people will never be called on to prove. Whatever your long-term challenges, your strength and courage are qualities of which you can feel justifiably proud.

Planning the future

Let's end this chapter on a positive note and look at long-term hopes. There are so many long-term hopes that it's impossible even to scratch the surface. For once, you have a future. You have a life you can look forward to and you can start to experience a sense of promise that you may not have felt in years.

Start to think of the future as beginning the very moment you wake in the morning without a hangover, a headache or without that dry-mouthed, pill-induced dullness invading your whole body. Everybody knows that waking up tired is a dreadful feeling but there was a time when that was routine for you. That was in the old days and, even if you don't wake up to the sun streaming through the bedroom window every morning, appreciate the sheer joy of having a productive day ahead of you.

Yes, you may have to go to work, to do the dishes from last night, to prepare breakfast and pack the children off to school, but think of all this as part of your new-found responsibilities as a clear-headed adult – and embrace them.

The following is a true story: Bryan had been divorced several years and who, on his own admission, never lifted a finger to help his then wife in the house. He relied on her to do the washing up, the washing, the cleaning and the ironing. Everything.

One day, post-divorce, he found himself alone in a new flat having to look after himself. He got up before his six-year-old son and went downstairs to iron some of his shirts. After half an hour or so, his son came into the kitchen and saw his dad standing in front of an ironing board with an iron in his hand. The young lad stopped dead in his tracks, his jaw dropped in surprise, and he said in pure astonishment, 'I've never seen you doing that before!'

'No', said Bryan. 'But you'll see me doing much more of it in the future.'

Bryan later admitted that he now actively enjoyed doing the chores. Not in the sense that he enjoyed ironing and washing in themselves, but he enjoyed the sense of taking responsibility for his own life. When he was married he realized he had been acting like a child, expecting everything to be done for him and taking responsibility for nothing. As a result, he was hardly a role model for his son who saw him effectively evading domestic chores and responsibilities. In his new role as an independent adult, Bryan took a real pride in caring for himself and was, as a result, a much more effective and conscientious father.

You, too, can start to take enjoyment and pride in all the little things that keep house and home together. Then transfer that attitude to work. This sense of pride and purpose, of doing all the little things well is a very effective way of filling the void that abstaining from drink, drugs or gambling has created.

Planning for the future is all about developing a new attitude of mind, a new outlook on life. Try to make a conscious effort to focus on the new and exciting things you can do rather than on the damaging things you've left behind. The opportunities now open to you are limitless. Write down all the things you'd like to do. Be as wild and unrealistic as you like. Write down dreams you had and dreams you still have; don't be embarrassed by them. Do you dream of climbing Everest, playing in the World Cup, becoming a Hollywood actress, standing for Parliament, walking to the North Pole or sailing the Atlantic? If, after a moment's thought, you realize you may be aiming a little too high, scale down your ambitions. What about fell walking, taking up five-aside, joining your local amateur dramatic society, becoming a local councillor, taking up the triathlon or joining a sailing club? Anything is possible if you really go for it. Take your list of dreams, tinker about with it, and come up with achievable goals that will give your new life meaning and purpose. It's a wide world out there and now you've become part of it again. Embrace it with enthusiasm and enjoy every second of your new non-addictive state.

Part 4:
Real Lives

All people are different; all addicts are the same. Addiction reduces everyone from whatever class, social background or income bracket to the same level of dependency. For the addict, all the differences, quirks and foibles of personality – all those characteristics that make every one of us unique – are shrouded in a heavy, suffocating blanket of need.

In the stories that follow, the experiences of people from many walks of life have been interwoven to show how lives become smaller and smaller until they contain nothing but drink, drugs, or gambling. Interests, hobbies, pastimes and pleasures slowly vanish as the addiction takes hold. Worse still, family, friends, partners and children become virtual strangers as the addict's one and only desperate relationship is with the bottle, pills or the racetrack.

This spiral of decline will be familiar to many of you. So, too, will be the moment when help was called for. From then on it becomes possible to reverse the downwards spiral and start to move upwards once again. Every day without a drink, a bet or a fix gives strength and makes the addict better able to rejoin the human race.

In these stories based on real experiences you will find despair and loss giving way to courage and hope. However low these men and women sank they found the strength to rise up again. You can take heart for two reasons. First, treatment is possible and you or someone close to you can be well again. Second, stories like these prove that **you are not alone**.

13

Shared stories and shared hopes

As a retired primary school teacher living on a pension in the home counties, I'm hardly the typical 'drug addict' but I realized two years ago that that was what I'd become. I'd been plagued by migraines for years and eventually my doctor prescribed some tablets that did the trick. The trouble was that I found I was taking more and more to achieve the same effect.

I didn't tell my doctor about this but instead made excuses for repeat prescriptions. I was terrified he would stop prescribing them. Once I even altered the number on one of the prescriptions which I then took to another pharmacy at the other side of town. I realized that not only was I physically dependent on the medication but that I was psychologically addicted and terrified of facing a day without the tablets.

I eventually plucked up courage to tell my doctor what I was doing. He was very kind and told me the dangers I was running if I continued to misuse the drugs as I was. We then agreed a carefully controlled and reduced dose which I've stuck to ever since.

Alice, 60, retired teacher

I started drinking heavily in my early twenties. Drink was just a part of the social scene. It was a world of pubs, clubs, wine bars, receptions, parties – all liberally provided with booze. I was drinking every day and extra at the weekends when I'd often wake up with tremendous headaches and only a vague recollection of what I'd been doing the night before.

Eventually the drinking began to control me and I found myself drinking earlier in the day and at lunchtimes, always making excuses for a celebration or a party. In truth there was no celebration at all because the only point of any party was to get drinking as soon as possible. Friends commented on how much I was drinking and I occasionally made half-hearted attempts to cut down. Never with much success. It never really bothered me because I was convinced I could handle it all.

Things came to a head for me when I woke up ill in a hotel room without the faintest idea of how I had got there. I was in a mess. I'd woken up fully clothed on top of the bed and gone straight to the bathroom to be sick. In fact when I checked the sheets I saw signs of vomit on them and realized I'd just crashed out at some point completely out of control.

It was a big shock and it was enough to send me straight off to Alcoholics Anonymous where I met people with similar tales of woe to tell. Stopping drinking was comparatively easy but staying stopped was a struggle. In the first few weeks, the temptation was quite intense but with support from friends (and from the new friends I was meeting) I managed to stay sober.

I've not had a drink now for three years and although I occasionally get a bit of a craving, it soon passes. I figure that what I've gained by giving up compensates for the loss of a drink. I have more energy and purpose in my life, I wake up clear-headed and enjoy the simple things in life rather than seeing everything through a haze of alcohol. It really is like a new life.

Ellen, 45, fashion buyer

I'm married with two children and look like a picture of normality. I get the kids ready for school, go to work, and come home for supper with my wife and family. During the day time, however, I am driven by the urge to bet: on the horses, the dogs, the pools, even who will score first in a Chelsea versus Manchester United match. All I have to see is a sign in the bookies saying 'Win £540 for £1' and I put a bet on. More often than not £10.

Over the past ten years I reckon I have spent upwards of £50,000 on gambling. A big win gives me a real buzz but only persuades me to put a bigger stake on the next race. If I lose I just think it's only a matter of time until I'm 'up' again. But I never am.

My wife and I have had endless arguments over my gambling and over the rocky state of our finances. I work hard but have little to show for it and I can understand how miserable she feels when she compares us with other members of the family who have the money for holidays and nice clothes and so on.

Six months ago she gave me an ultimatum. I had to choose between the family or the gambling. She had threatened to leave many times but this time I felt she was serious. She said unless I got professional help she would leave me and take the children with her.

I signed up to Gamblers Anonymous and began working through my problems with a counsellor. Having the support of people who knew how I behaved and who understood what was driving me was an enormous help. With their help, I've not had a bet for over six months and my relationship with my wife has improved no end. I can't say it's been easy and there are times I get a real twinge of temptation. But I'm determined to see it through.

Sam, 35, Information Technology (IT) manager

I don't know how I got into heavy drinking really. Or, at least, I'm not sure when social drinking tipped into heavy drinking. There was always alcohol around in my work. There were farewell do's or some excuse for the wine to come out practically every week. Drinking after work was routine. It was even encouraged. We all just piled into the bar and had three or four pints and then went on for meals with wine and spirits.

My wife complained a bit in the early years of our marriage but I was young, ambitious, and wanted to keep in with the crowd and she sort of grudgingly understood I had to be out with the lads. But it started to escalate after about five years into the job. I'd come home absolutely legless and no way could I try to say this was work related.

It started to get worse and worse and I'd use interviews as excuses to get a spot of lunchtime drinking in as well. I'd arrange to meet people for long lunches and, all on expenses of course, order a couple of bottles minimum. I'd get back to the office reasonably in control (so I thought) and bash out my copy just in time for an evening session that could last until closing time.

Anyway, my wife had an affair (not surprising really) and I went downhill big time. She eventually left me and my professional life went into meltdown. I'd turn up at work reeking of drink and, although nobody said anything to me at the time, I later discovered I'd become a bit of a joke in the newsroom. Fortunately I had a boss who'd been an alcoholic himself and he took me to one side and gave me an ultimatum. Either I get myself off to Alcoholics Anonymous (AA) or I'd get the bullet.

I did what he said and slowly changed my life around. Not that it was easy. It wasn't. Even today, five years after I admitted I was an alcoholic, I can get terrible pangs when I see groups of young men and women laughing and joking over wine and beer on a summer's evening on the outdoor terrace of a city pub.

I resist, though. I got married again two years ago and my wife and I have a lovely daughter. I wouldn't jeopardize that for the world. My relationship is stronger than any craving I get. I got one chance. I won't get another.

Guy, 48, journalist

My boyfriend, Dan, who's the same age as me, has always smoked cannabis since I got to know him at university. He was in a band and wrote his own songs and the drugs seemed to go with the territory. I didn't really approve but I accepted it was part of his lifestyle. Unusually he doesn't drink (I do in moderation). So while I would relax over a glass or two of white wine he would light up a joint.

The arrangement worked well enough, even though I couldn't help feeling that he was becoming more taciturn and strangely distant when we were together. While I became a bit more animated after a glass of wine and wanted to talk more, he seemed to retreat into himself and didn't really seem to respond to the conversation. I found I was getting less back from him somehow. It's hard to explain but he seemed to be only half there at times.

A year ago, however, his use increased dramatically, and not only is he now smoking more he's smoking more often. At weekends he will start by mid-morning. I raised this with him and at first he brushed things aside. But when I tackled him about his huge mood swings – between hyperactivity and blank depression – he agreed to cut down. It didn't last for long though and soon he was back to his high consumption. We began communicating less, our sex life tailed off to next to nothing, and I began to get seriously worried.

I have a really good relationship with my mum who's a nurse and I raised some of my fears with her. She said he should really get himself some treatment and she even came over to chat to both of us about it. He got really defensive about it and said it was a harmless lifestyle choice. The conversation ended civilly (just) but Dan clearly didn't want to do anything about it.

Things came to a head six months ago when I decided I'd had enough of living with someone who wasn't 'there' most of the time. I went to live with my mum for a few weeks before I found another place to rent.

I'm still really fond of Dan and it hurts me to see him going downhill. I go round and we talk and I try to get through to him but it's just impossible. I can't see how our relationship is going to survive this. I decided there was nothing more I could do myself and I had to accept that until he wants to give up his drug habit there's very little any of us can do.

Bella, 27, teacher

After my second child was born ten years ago, I suffered from a bout of postnatal depression. I'd never been really ill before so I was reluctant to see the doctor over what I thought was just a blip in my frame of mind. I'd been told that some mothers do feel bad after pregnancy but, as I'd not experienced it with my first, I didn't really realize what was happening.

The doctor prescribed a course of antidepressants and I just took them. I did feel much better in some ways but quite strange in others and I didn't really like the way they made me feel. I sort of felt 'drugged up' all the time. Anyway I carried on taking them and even agreed to another course and another. I'd no idea that legally prescribed drugs could have such an addictive effect.

I tried to come off them but I found I felt really bad, and I kept on taking them just to get some relief. I'd feel sick and achey all the time without them. I couldn't sleep, I felt tired all day, and I had to give up my part-time work and stay at home.

It took me the best part of five years to come off them and that was only because I read in a magazine that prescription drugs could be addictive. I was horrified to think I was some sort of drug addict and I blamed myself for getting in such a state. At one point, my weight had dropped to 38 kg (6 stone) and I looked – and felt – terrible.

My own doctor retired and a new younger doctor took over. After I'd explained how I felt and told her my story she recognized the symptoms straightaway and immediately put me on a course of drugs. She was very open with me and very understanding, but she was also quite firm and told me I was not to take more of the tablets than she had prescribed and that, as the dosage got less and less, I should be prepared to stop at a certain time.

When I eventually did I stop, felt much better. There was severe discomfort at first but the doctor explained that this would pass and that under no circumstances should I go back to the old drugs. Even with the discomfort, though, I felt more myself than I had done and eventually I resumed a normal life. But those 5 years were very hard and I shudder when I think back to them.

Josephine, 40, part-time secretary and homemaker

I used to play rugby as a young man, and a match was always followed by a drinking session that lasted all evening. It was enjoyable and, although I and others got drunk, it had an innocent quality to it that at the time didn't seem to be much of a problem. I rarely drank in the week so a weekend blow-out, especially after all the exercise, seemed OK.

Then I had a bad car accident that put me in hospital for a couple of months and ended my playing career. I went down to the club every week as usual but stood on the sidelines cheering the team on. I was still accepted as one of the lads and I still joined in the drinking sessions afterwards. But gradually I could feel myself drinking more and more seriously. It was as if all the carefree innocence had evaporated and I was drinking to blot something out.

I'd taken the accident quite badly and it was only with the support of my wife and friends that I managed to get back into a social life at all. Yet somehow, as I said, all the fun had gone out of my social sessions and I found myself drinking on my own as well as at the club. I started going out after work for four or five pints and would come home and have a few whiskies before (and after) dinner.

My wife commented on my drinking patterns but nothing really changed. In fact it got worse; I took to drinking during the day and even keeping a bottle of scotch in my locker in the print shop. I used to fill a hip flask from it and would pour little tots into my tea throughout the day.

Back home, I'd stay up after my wife had gone to bed and polish off the best part of a bottle of scotch most nights. Things came to a head in two ways. Not only was I putting on a lot of weight after being quite fit but my wife complained that I was spending far too much money on drink. We sat down and talked about it and I agreed to cut down – which I did for a couple of weeks. But then my dad died and everything seemed to go downhill after that.

Forget slowing down; I stepped it up. Solitary drinking became the norm. I virtually ignored my wife in the evening and our married life was in a terrible mess. As was my life in general. I'd stagger up to bed at around two or three and crash out until seven when I woke up feeling and looking dreadful. I managed to make it into work but I'm sure everybody could see from my appearance that all was not well. By lunchtime I'd perked up a bit and was ready for a couple of liveners at the bar instead of anything substantial to eat. That pattern lasted for about two or three years. I don't know how I survived really.

Things came to a head when I took a day off work because my hangover was so bad I could hardly move. By evening, I was still in bed when my wife came home. She hit the roof when I finally surfaced at about seven o'clock and immediately poured myself another whisky.

Then she burst into tears and stormed out of the house. I don't remember a thing after that until 36 hours later when I woke up with a terrible hangover which I initially thought was the hangover from the previous day. I was about to phone in sick when I looked at all the bottles on the table and on the floor and something stopped me. I realized I'd spent a whole day at home drinking on my own. I'd been off work two days now and both of them lost to drink.

This frightened me and I phoned my wife who I knew would be at her mum's. We talked things over and I agreed to go to Alcoholics Anonymous (AA). It wasn't easy giving up but

I had a very understanding counsellor who talked me through some of the reasons I'd taken to the bottle. With AA's support and the backing of my wife, I got through and am now running my own printing business. The episode was about 20 years ago. I haven't touched a drop since but I don't take things for granted. I take every day as it comes and thank my lucky stars for it.

David, 47, printer

My mother was an alcoholic for 20 years. Her drinking started, I seem to remember, about the time my sister and I started secondary school. Dad left when we were very young and I remember dreading coming home for fear of what state she'd be in. Just hearing her slurring her words as I came in through the door was one of the worst things. That sound is still with me now and if I ever hear anybody speak like that I feel physically ill and want to walk away.

The drinking got progressively worse although there were times when she seemed to be a normal mother to us. She'd go for a couple of days without drinking and would behave like a normal mother making food for us and even baking cakes. Those periods were like bursts of sunshine between the rain. Pretty soon, though, the clouds would start to form again and Mum was at the sherry. Then at the wine. Then at the whisky.

'Polly' and I would watch telly with her but we soon became so uncomfortable with her constantly drinking that we went upstairs to do our homework. Eventually we persuaded Mum to buy a TV for the two of us and we used to go up into Polly's room and watch it together rather than stay downstairs with Mum slowly drinking herself senseless. Eventually it was if we were living two separate lives.

Needless to say we never brought anybody back to the house. We were too ashamed to do that. Too ashamed of our mum, which was terrible. Occasionally, Granny would come round with Mum's sister but we were never allowed to hear what they said. We were shooed out of the room while inside you could hear raised voices and sometimes crying.

I couldn't wait to leave home and get a job just to get out of the house. By this time, there was no communication between us. I mean, I loved Mum, and I still do but I couldn't get through to her. I told her she needed help and *she said she'd get it but she never did. When I got married she turned up at the church visibly the worse for wear and got into a dreadful state at the reception. In fact my auntie had to take her away.*

When we eventually had kids I wondered about taking them to see her. It didn't matter too much when they were very young (though I couldn't let them play on the floor because the place was so filthy). But now they've grown up a bit I just don't want to take them round. I don't want them to be as ashamed of their granny as I was of my mum. I go round to tidy up once a week but really I can't wait to leave.

The trouble is I feel so guilty. I hate myself for it and I find myself crying at work for no reason, which is very embarrassing when you're serving customers. Fortunately a friend at the bank put me in touch with Al-Anon, an organization for the family of alcoholics. It's been a huge relief frankly to know that I'm not alone. I really look forward to those meetings. Everyone is so friendly and understanding. It's like a big family in a way. I still feel guilty and I'm having to work through it but at least I've stopped crying at work. Which is a start.

Sarah, 33, bank clerk

I'm in real trouble but I just can't stop myself. I spend all my money on gambling. The horses and the casino mainly. I've spent all my student grant easily by half term and I'm keeping on two jobs just to feed my habit. I don't eat much, I don't smoke and I'm as thin as a rake, largely, I think, because of all the nervous energy I expend on this compulsive betting.

It started after some friends and I went for a day out to the races. We all decided to spend £20 just on betting and be ready to lose it if necessary. It was all part of the fun. The deal was that we gave half of any winnings back to the kitty. By an astonishing stroke of luck I ended up winning £400. I was over the moon and we all went out for a great meal on the proceeds afterwards.

The trouble was that I immediately got the taste for it even though, as far as I know, none of my friends have been near a racetrack or a betting shop ever again. I started to study the form and bet about £5 twice a week. That soon escalated to nearer £5 a day then £10. I'd put more on if I managed something like a decent win.

I found I was spending longer and longer at the bookies. Instead of going in, watching a race, and coming out, I'd stay in for hours at a time working out complicated permutations of bets which sometimes brought in some decent money. Overall though, I soon realized any money I had was, over time, just going into the bookies' pockets. Not that it stopped me. I kept on betting and betting like a madman, eventually going into debt and borrowing from my parents.

I sold my laptop and my CD player to get betting money and was completely abandoning my studies. My tutor gave me a telling off one day for consistently failing to hand in work. When I told him I had money problems and was having to work to pay for myself he seemed sympathetic – though I'm sure he wouldn't have been if I'd told him where the money was going.

I've started to work a bit more but I do it at night when I've finished at the restaurant. I'm up until late, then I go to a lecture or two, then I'm down at the betting shop all afternoon. I'm going mental. Six months ago I started going to a casino in the city, in fact I wangled myself a job behind the bar which I thought was great.

*Trouble is I feel like a nervous wreck.
I know I should get down to work more but all
I can think of is gambling. I'd heard of
Gamblers' Anonymous and I've been along to a
few meetings. There are some nice guys there
who are trying to help me. One in particular is
not much older than me and we've got quite
friendly. I'm going to carry on going and I hope
eventually to manage my problem, but at the
moment I just can't seem to help myself.*

Barry, 21, student

*For as long as I can remember Mum used to
drink. My parents seemed to lead entirely
separate lives, with Dad taking himself off
most evenings to council meetings or committee
meetings or whatever. He was always making
excuses to stay out of the house and left me
with Mum who used to struggle just to make a
meal for us. She'd make something like pasta
but never seemed to eat any of hers. Instead,
she'd have a bottle of wine on the table,
refilling her glass all the time. I didn't say
much about it because I'd no real idea what
was going on. I'd go up to my room and do
homework or listen to music.*

Eventually Dad must have had enough because one day he just left. Mum tried to give up drinking, I think, but it never seemed to last for long. The worst thing for me was coming home from school dreading what state she'd be in. I used to hope and pray she'd be sober and make me something nice to eat just like my friends' mothers.

Sometime I was lucky but mostly I would open the door, step into the living room and see her either slumped in front of the TV with a drink or sprawled out on the sofa asleep.

I had a very nice drama teacher at the time who suspected something was amiss at home. I developed quite a close relationship with her because I really felt comfortable in her company. She'd just listen and let me do all the talking, occasionally suggesting things I could do to make things better. She was the one who suggested to me that I should have a word with Mum about her drinking and she even came home with me once to have a word with her herself.

Mum took it very well actually and agreed that she'd better do something. Whatever she did do didn't seem to work that well, however, and she was soon back to the old ways. I just learned to accept it and not to say anything about it anymore. I suppose I buried it quite deep. Talking to my teacher was very important. She used to invite me to her home quite a lot where she and her husband used to cook meals for me. They'd take me out to some of their social and family gatherings and I became one of the family myself in the end.

I think the two of them were my lifelines really. I got into a routine of staying at school as long as I could then going home and just going straight to my room to work. Mum and I started to lead completely separate lives. I put all my effort into work and got good A Levels and a university place.

Life's pretty good at the moment now I'm living away from home – although I often feel guilty about Mum. There's not much I can do. I've suggested Alcoholics Anonymous but she seems pretty half-hearted about it. It's very sad. Liz (my former drama teacher) and her husband Luke are more like family now.

David, 22, student

*You wouldn't think so but there are lots of
heavy drinkers in my profession. Alcoholism, if
not an occupational hazard, is certainly very
common. But we tend to hide it quite well. Or I
certainly thought I did, at least from the outside
world if not from my family. My wife suspected
I had a problem, I'm sure, but we didn't really
discuss it. I was very successful, living in a
lovely house, earning lots of money. We had
two small children, took nice holidays and
everything seemed fine. The drinking I put
down to letting off steam after long days and
stressful cases.*

*I drank every evening without fail. A
couple of pints after work, a couple of G and Ts
before supper at home and a bottle of wine with
the meal – most of which I consumed myself.
Then almost certainly another bottle that I'd
finish after the meal. Weekends, parties and
celebrations were the worst though, when quite
often I'd get pretty near legless. In fact, I
remember one Christmas drinking so much
during the day that I could hardly see straight
to cook the turkey and my wife had to take over
while I collapsed on the sofa with a few black
looks from my parents who were staying with
us. No possibility of conversation, of course,*

*just chewing through the meal until we'd
finished the Christmas pudding and sat in front
of the TV – with another drink in my hand
of course.*

*I think, now I look back, that we were all
in denial about it and hoped, if we brushed it
under the proverbial carpet, it would go away.
After all, we were the perfect family. I loved
my wife and children and during the daytime
everything seemed hunky dory.*

*Luckily I had a boss who noticed. He'd
been round to the house for supper a couple of
times and had seen for himself how I could
shift it. In fact he did mention it once but I
brushed it all aside telling him I did drink a lot
but not as much as some people I knew! Which
was true. But it was when I routinely started to
come into the office smelling of drink that he
really became concerned and he asked me into
his office one day for a talk.*

*My work was suffering and he'd noticed,
and he noticed too that I was coming in looking
the worse for wear – despite the shower and the
immaculate suit and tie. Things came to a head
when I met him in our car park after quite a
heavy session with some friends. He confronted
me as I was about to get in the car and said*

*categorically that if I got into the car and
attempted to drive he'd call the police and I'd
be fired on the spot.*

*I got a taxi home feeling rather chastened
but also hard done by. Next day he gave it to
me straight. I had to see a doctor and stop
drinking or I'd be out of a job. That brought me
up with a start but I agreed.*

*My wife was relieved, I think, and I took
myself off to my doctor's and told him how
much I was drinking. Or, rather, I didn't. He
could see I was underplaying and he asked me
straight. How much? I told him, and in that
moment both of us knew the truth. I needed
help. The firm paid for treatment in a private
clinic and after a bit of arguing that I was fine
and didn't need it I checked in.*

*I'm not the 'worst' alcoholic people might
have seen but I came to realize that an
alcoholic is an alcoholic and although they
may all look and behave differently, they're
suffering from the same disease. It was difficult
at first getting used to a drink-free lifestyle but
I soon realized the alternative was far worse. I
suppose I was saved in the nick of time.*

Andrew, 50, lawyer

My first experience of a casino was when my fiancé, 'Colin', took me to one with a few of his friends for someone's birthday celebration. It was a jolly night out but a couple of people commented on the fact that I hadn't joined in at all. For some reason, I plonked myself down at one of the slot machines and kept feeding it money all night. I'd allowed myself £50 to spend and I spent it all – despite having two or three considerable wins.

I found it absolutely mesmerizing watching the drums spin and lining up before my eyes. And I found the ker-chung ker-chung sound of a winning line so exciting that I just wanted to play and play. A win gave me the encouragement to play more, and a loss gave me the determination to play more in order to get back what I'd put in. Looking back on it, I can see that the psychology behind it all is as clever as it is damaging.

All the time I was playing I was in my own little bubble. While the drums were spinning, Colin and his friends might just as well not have existed. In fact one of his friends jokingly said afterwards I was like 'a woman possessed'. How right he was.

Colin's work took him away on business for quite a lot of the month and, as I was studying at home, I often felt at a loose end in the evenings. Then one night I suggested to a girlfriend a trip to the casino. It was a bit of a disaster because, just like before, I sat at the machines and hardly spoke to her all night. She had to drag me away and, over a drink at the bar, made it clear this wasn't her sort of night out. Unfortunately, I had acquired a taste for it.

I went back to the casino more and more often, spending whole evenings there on my own and once even winning £15,000 at roulette! It was the best thing – but also the worst thing – that could have happened because it just fuelled an addiction that I was in complete denial about. Gambling was taking over my life.

Things came to a head when I admitted to my fiancé one evening that all the money I'd won a year earlier I had in fact now spent. He was terribly disappointed because we were both hoping to use the money for the wedding and the honeymoon. But then I had to tell him that not only had I lost the money I was a further £8,000 in debt. I'll never forget the look on his *face. It was one of disappointment, hurt, and a complete sense of betrayal.*

When he told me he was going to have to call off the wedding I was devastated and I pleaded with him to give me one more chance. I agreed to get help and, thanks to Gamblers Anonymous and Colin's patience, I've managed, touch wood, to turn myself around. Thanks to their advice, I've taken up running and go to an evening class once a week to learn Spanish. I've also joined a local choir and enjoy the company of friends rather than my solitary evenings at the casino.

I give my credit and debit cards to Colin whenever I don't need them for a shopping expedition or whatever and we now have a joint account that I know he can monitor any time he wants to. All these are practical strategies I learned from Gamblers Anonymous, and they seem to work as I haven't gambled a penny for almost a year now.

Jill, 24, student nurse

You can earn quite a bit as a plumber these days in London. I'm never out of a job. But ask my wife whether she ever saw any of my money and she'll give you a right mouthful. I just threw it all away on the horses, on the dogs, on the pools, on the scratchcards even.

All my wages would go on gambling. After work, at lunchtime, even during work on the mobile to the bookies. Ten pounds, fifty pounds, a hundred pounds, sometimes more. I'd just about get by with the wife if I had a big win. I once cleared £15,000 on a four horse accumulator. That got me in credit with her for a while. She took a big slice of it for the housekeeping. Just as well really because I wasn't tipping up anything at the end of the week for months on end. We were living off our savings – well her savings really. We'd have these almighty rows about money and about how she was at the end of her tether with me. Loads of times she threatened to leave but somehow she always managed to stay.

Then she got breast cancer and was in and out of hospital for quite a while. I'd go up and see her of course but I would always be fitting it in around going to the bookies. I was winning a bit but losing a hell of a lot and I remember saying I'd got a letter saying they were going to cut the telephone off. My wife was furious, well, as furious as she could be in her state, because she always paid the bills on time and hated to be in debt. When I told her that the gas people were threatening to do the same she just started crying. I felt terrible.

There she was really ill and there I was adding to the misery. I couldn't help it though. I was just chasing my losses hoping for a big win to wipe all the trouble away. My wife eventually had an operation and when she came back home things went very quiet. We hardly ever spoke except to just pass the time of day. It was like walking on glass. Then one evening she said she was going to leave me. Just like that. No shouting, no words, no raised voices. I knew she meant it.

She explained why and for the first time in my life I felt I was going to lose everything. I had no idea what to do. I phoned round a few people, most of them gambling mates, and got no joy. Then a chap from the local church knocked on the door handing out leaflets. We sort of got talking and in the end I found myself admitting everything to him.

He saved my life really. He mentioned Gamblers Anonymous and told me how to contact them. In fact, he was there when I dialled them. I can't say I attend his church much – it's not my sort of thing – but I try to show my face at Christmas. He still comes round to get me though. And thanks to him and the organization I haven't had a bet in 18 months. Fingers crossed. And me and the wife are getting on better than ever.

Jim, 56, plumber

I'd been addicted to gambling for about ten years without admitting it to myself. I'd been a regular at the bookies since leaving school but as I started to get a bit of money behind me I found myself betting larger and larger amounts. And of course losing larger and larger amounts. It was a real buzz when I won and I convinced myself I was recouping what I'd lost. Over time, though, I was always down.

That's when things went into real decline because I'd raise the stake to get myself back into the black. I once bet £1,000 on a 5–1 'certainty'. It lost. And for the first time I realized I was in trouble, but I didn't do anything about it. I just put it down to experience and carried on with my old ways.

Meanwhile, my gambling was playing havoc with my home life. I'd have rows with my wife, I was forever shouting at the kids for no reason at all, and I was getting increasingly wound up and on edge. It was only when I sat down and saw that I was £22,000 in debt that I realised I was in a big hole. And that was the reason for my constant irritability.

I sat down with my wife and had a long chat. We discussed some pretty deep stuff, I can tell you, and I was forced to confront what was definitely an addiction. We agreed I would stop betting and get some proper help – which was when I went to Gamblers Anonymous. I immediately felt I was with people who could understand my compulsion, and knowing I wasn't the only one in this mess was an immense relief. I came clean with the bank and between us we came up with a repayment plan. It's got some way to go yet but at least I can see things steadily improving month by month. It's much better than seeing my money (and my life) going down the plughole.

Alan, 34, builder

Part 5:
Staying Free

The challenge is often not so much quitting as continuing to abstain. It's less about giving up the drink, the drugs or the gambling lifestyle and more about the lifelong commitment to abstinence. This is not always an easy thing to do, but millions of men and women have proved that it is possible. In this final section, we provide you with some straightforward maintenance advice to help to keep you strong and free of your old addictions for good and to help consolidate what you've picked up so far.

14

Maintenance
techniques

Relaxation

We all think we know what we mean by relaxing. Kicking off your shoes, opening a bar of chocolate, and sprawling on the sofa with a magazine or a DVD. Well, this is true up to a point. There's no doubt that's one way of winding down, but deep relaxation involves more than that and it doesn't come quite so easily, it needs to be practised.

Deep relaxation isn't about taking a rest or putting your feet up. It's designed to revive you, yes, but it does so without the excess of sensory stimulation that can often be far from relaxing. Think of the DVD and the chocolates, for example. Clearly, if you're watching a nail-biting thriller, your adrenalin levels (boosted by the rush of sugar from the chocolate) are going to be quite high. Although you're not working, you're certainly not relaxing either. Strangely enough, even though the experience is pleasurable, your body is technically under quite a lot of stress. It's like being on a white-knuckle ride at the theme park – great fun and excitement but hardly relaxation.

Proper relaxation, far from being mere entertainment and enjoyment, is a therapeutic technique with the aim of bringing about an actual change in your mood and behaviour. It usually involves one or more of the following elements:

- Silence

- Concentration

- Meditation

- Stillness

- Controlled breathing.

Why should you relax?

When you were in your addictive state, you were constantly ruled by your feelings, which would overwhelm rational thought and leave you enslaved to aroused emotions. Relaxation is the opposite of this. If you find yourself wrestling with a craving or subject to negative emotions like anger, or frustration, tension or disappointment, relaxation can help restore your peace of mind and equilibrium.

Relaxation helps you to bring down stress levels, which in themselves could be the danger signals triggering a return to your old patterns of behaviour. Yet silence and concentration in this busy, noisy world are not easy to find. You'll need to make the time and the space in your life for them. Once you've done that, you'll be amazed at the results. The rewards of deep relaxation are certainly worthwhile.

Making time and space

Let's say you sleep for eight hours and you work for eight hours. That means you have a further eight hours left over for whatever you choose. Can you find half an hour, say, in which to clear your thoughts in a silent and stress-free environment?

You might prefer to find a quiet spot somewhere as soon as you get up, or after breakfast, at lunchtime, or when you get home from work. Although not ideal, you could even try to cultivate a bubble of silence on the bus or train to work. Close your eyes but resist the urge to fall asleep. Keep quite wakeful and try to blot out the noise all around you while you concentrate on a thought or an image. It's a strange sensation at first but one you will find quite rewarding after a little practice.

Choose a favourite part of your house or flat that isn't used as a thoroughfare by anyone else, and try to make it your own. Place some flowers, perhaps, or a picture or photograph where you can see it, and try to make that space your own, your little haven and sanctuary for half an hour. If this conjures up some weird and wacky 1960s style meditation with joss sticks and sitars, it's not meant to. This relaxation technique is just as easy to do in the greenhouse or in the shed – in fact, anywhere you can be alone with yourself and your thoughts.

If undisturbed space isn't easy to find at home, try to find a spot elsewhere that you can make your own. For example, in the park, by the lake or under a shady tree, in the library, in your local church or in a big cathedral. You can relax in an art gallery, say, or a museum – anywhere you can escape for just a moment from the hustle and bustle of everyday life and have some quiet time to yourself.

Breathing

So you've made the time and found the space. What next? The first stage is to be comfortable. If sitting, uncross your legs and sit comfortably with your hands on your lap. Try to wear loose clothing – a fleece and tracksuit bottoms are perfect at home. Go barefoot or wear socks without shoes. If you choose to lie down, place a small pillow under your head for support and either fold your arms on your chest or hold them palms downwards by your side. Obviously, if you're choosing a public space, lying down or even sitting barefoot may not be possible. In that case, just make do with what you have.

Next, be aware of the weight of your arms and hands and feel the pressure of your feet on the floor. Get comfortable – but not so comfortable that you're tempted to nod off! Now you're ready for the next stage: controlled breathing.

The key to successful relaxation is controlling your breathing. Start to breathe in slowly and rhythmically and then to breathe out for longer than you inhaled. You might like to count as you breathe, making the breath in last five seconds and the breath out last seven. Do this 10 or 20 times, all the time concentrating only on your breaths in and out, in and out. With each cycle of breathing you'll find your whole body noticeably releasing, allowing calm and peace to take the place of stress and tension.

If half an hour is too much for you, break it down into two sessions of 15 or maybe just 10 minutes. You'll be surprised how much you can achieve in a relatively short space of time.

Another method of relaxing involves lying down comfortably and feeling the weight of all your limbs pressing on the floor. While continuing to breathe rhythmically feel the weight of your right foot, then your right leg, then concentrate on the weight of your left foot and your left leg, moving up the body and being aware of the pressure on the small of your back, your chest and your head. Listen to the silence which, after a few moments, will be not so silent as you thought. Concentrate on the slightest creak or sound in the room, listen to the distant birdsong or the faraway hum of the traffic. It's in the slow, rhythmic breathing and the act of concentration that you'll begin to achieve a deep sense of relaxation.

Try also to develop peace and calm as an attitude of mind. Try to feel calm even in the most hectic of locations by controlling your breathing as outlined above. Try to feel that, for the moment, your own body is the entire world and that all the other noises of the train, the bus or the street are on the outside. Paradoxically, large public spaces can be good for this. While they're anything but quiet they give you the opportunity to imagine yourself in your own bubble of peacefulness – a haven entirely of your own making.

Some people find relaxation tapes useful for inducing this mood of calm. They use a soft repetitive melody, often incorporating natural sounds such as waves breaking on the shore, trees rustling in the breeze or wind chimes tinkling in the air. If you choose one with a wave theme, for example, try imagining yourself on that distant beach with water lapping gently around your feet. The possibilities are endless. Go where your imagination takes you, all the while breathing deeply and rhythmically. Even ten minutes' relaxation can revive you enormously and, crucially, get you over a vulnerable period when the stress seems to be building up dangerously.

Maintaining a sense of purpose

A sense of purpose is fundamental to well-being. It's important in everyone's life, but more so in the life of a recovering addict. Surprisingly, many people, if they were honest, would say they don't have any real sense of purpose and get by from day to day repetitively going to work, coming home, switching on the telly, and perhaps taking a fortnight's holiday once a year. If they find themselves in a state of boredom or emptiness they can always have a drink or a smoke to give them a temporary high which they feel will get them over the blankness. Then back to the same old routine. This option is not open to you. Artificial highs are no longer possible, and any highs you achieve will have to be of the natural type, the highs that last. Life's natural highs are largely to be found in relationships: a healthy relationship with yourself and a positive and fulfilling relationship with others.

Self

Try to be at ease in your own skin, changing what you can and accepting what you can't. Work on a personal audit, a kind of mental, emotional, and perhaps spiritual check on your hopes and aspirations. Your goals don't need to be grand, just geared to your own personality and needs.

Reward yourself with a gong in an imaginary New Year's honours list! Look at what you've achieved in life – from bringing up children to being a hard worker – and give yourself an honorary award. In honours terms, you may not be the captain of industry, the theatrical celebrity or the ground breaking surgeon honoured for their contribution to the economy, the arts or sciences, but you may be the dinner lady who's changed the school menu and got the kids eating healthily again, the police constable who's valued as a stalwart of community policing, the foster mother who, with no expectation of recognition or reward, has transformed the lives of dozens of children. In short, recognize and reward yourself for being your own ordinary self, capable of doing the ordinary things in life exceptionally well. That's certainly worth a gong.

Others

By now you'll know better than most that you're not an island. Whether a carer or an ex-addict, you have needed the support of other people to survive. Begin to transform your need for others into an active desire to work with and help other people yourself.

Try to connect with people on as many levels as you can, taking an active interest in the parent-teachers' association of your child's school, for example, or doing voluntary work with a charity of your choice. At Christmas, which may be a great strain for you, think of lending a helping hand with the organization Crisis. Crisis exists to help men and women sleeping on the streets (many of them also alcoholics or drug users) get warm food and clean clothing. No alcohol or drugs are allowed on the premises so there will be no danger of temptation. On the contrary, by keeping yourself busy with all the mundane tasks of preparing food, serving it and clearing up, you'll be occupying all your spare time while at the same time contributing to a worthwhile cause. And who knows who you might meet? You could make a lifelong friend or you could, with a word of encouragement based on your own experience, be the person that opens the door just a fraction for someone else in need – long enough to encourage an alcoholic or drug abuser to take the first steps on their own road to recovery. Anything can happen if you allow it to.

These small actions of community involvement will give you the ongoing encouragement to be strong and the solid conviction that you're part of a world that can be endured without resorting to artificial chemicals and dangerous patterns of behaviour.

Support networks

These exist in many different forms and can be found in many different places. Alcoholics Anonymous, for instance, has long pioneered the sponsor system – the idea of assigning a successfully recovering alcoholic the task of overseeing and monitoring the recovery of another more recent and inexperienced member. At its simplest, a support network need involve only one other person.

Sponsors

These could turn out to be your guardian angels, and stories abound of the deep bonds of respect and affection that grow between recovering addicts and their sponsors. It takes effort, commitment and a genuine sense of selflessness to help a fellow human being in this way, and sponsors are to be cherished and applauded. However, remember that not only do you have a responsibility to yourself (and, if you have them, to your dependants), you also have a responsibility not to let your sponsors down.

You must be sincere in your desire to change. Simply promising to cut down, to give up tomorrow or next week, to have just the one, is not good enough. Each time you slide, your sponsor will suffer personal disappointment and may even be tempted to shoulder some of the blame. Inflicting those feelings on someone who is trying to help you is simply not fair. Before agreeing to the care of a sponsor, talk through all the implications, be honest about your ultimate intentions, and promise to keep your side of whatever bargain you agree.

Friends

In the absence of (or perhaps in addition to) a formal sponsor, think about asking a friend or a family member to keep an eye on you. It's a lot to ask, but if you keep your side of the bargain it could be the beginning of a healing partnership. Because it is a lot to ask, we would suggest that, having first been honest about your condition and your intentions, you mutually agree a time limit on the term of sponsorship. With some friends it might be a month; with others six months.

If you find yourself constantly relapsing and making repeated promises to start again, it may not be time to ask anyone other than a formal sponsor to take the responsibility of watching over you.

Before you take such a serious step and enlist the help of a friend, that friend will need to have clear evidence of your determination to alter the pattern of your behaviour. It is not fair to land them with the repeated disappointment and frustration that flow from your partial resolve. It's all or nothing.

If you're in a loving relationship with another (however bruised you've made it or allowed it to become), then he or she will have given you their support over what has probably been a very long time. With each promise broken, with each drink or self-medication with tablets, or loss at the bookies you will have been testing that support to destruction. Remember, we are all only human and your long-suffering partner deserves an end to the heartache and disappointment that stem from your repeated relapses. If you ask for support again you must be certain you can do your bit (lot) to meet them at least half way.

Groups

Group support is immensely helpful. The presence of people who've been through similar experiences to you offers reassurance and real comfort. Moreover, being able to admit your vulnerability to a group of friendly strangers, to open up and maybe to break down in an environment of complete safety is a source of healing.

Organizations like Alcoholics and Gamblers Anonymous can give professional expertise that has been established over decades and their care and compassion are second to none. These should be early ports of call if you seriously want to quit damaging patterns of behaviour. If you haven't yet accessed their services, you should really make the effort to try them out. You may be initially reluctant or shy, even embarrassed or ashamed at the prospect of standing in front of your peers (or youngers or elders) and admitting things you've kept hidden in the darkest recesses of your heart. If you take the plunge, rest assured that the welcome will be open, sincere and non-judgemental. You have nothing to lose and everything to gain.

Once you've joined, continue to keep up your membership. That way you too may be able to offer, in time, your services as a sponsor and friend to those newly signing up. In doing so you'll discover a new sense of purpose in your life and take on a new responsibility to yourself and others – all of which will conspire to keep you strong and free.

Carers and dependants

Carers need support, too. There are groups and individuals who possess the insight to know that alcohol, drugs, and gambling can corrode not only the lives of addicts but of those closest to them as well. We admire the men and women whose compassion extends to those innocents caught up unintentinally in the web of addiction.

Remember that carers can use helplines. At the end of the book we list addresses and phone numbers that you, as a carer, can access. Just as an addict can feel ashamed of his or her behaviour and fight shy of contacting an organization you may feel ashamed that your partner, friend, brother, sister, son or daughter is an addict. Please, please, don't feel ashamed or guilty. You will be welcomed without judgement, condemnation or blame. You will be in safe and healing hands.

Alcohol

Al-Anon is a tremendous resource for families and friends of problem drinkers. They offer support and advice sometimes long after the problem drinking has stopped or after the problem drinker has disappeared from the scene.

It's thought that an alcoholic will affect the lives of at least four people within his or her circle of friends and family. Al-Anon works on the principle that alcoholism is a family disease. Alateen is part of Al-Anon and, as its name suggests, specializes in providing support for teenagers affected by an adult's drinking – usually one or both parents.

The National Association for Children of Alcoholics (NACOA) is an independent charity set up to help not only the younger members of a family affected by problem drinking but also those men and women who have reached adulthood but are still affected by the patterns of alcoholism (usually by parents) in their formative years. It recognizes that even when children have left home and long after the problem drinking has become a regular feature of their daily life, those affected in childhood can go on to suffer from a range of emotional and physical problems.

Drugs

A National Drugs Helpline exists to provide help and advice to those affected by drugs and substance abuse. It's also known as 'Talk to Frank', providing, as its name suggests, free, clear, independent and honest advice on a one-to-one basis with a guarantee of complete anonymity.

Adfam is a national charity helping families affected by drugs (including alcohol). It is one of the leading agencies in the UK specializing in the family implications of drug abuse and acts as a forum for the free exchange of advice and support.

Addaction began life 40 years ago as an association of parents of addicts. It works closely with drug abusers and their families and friends as well as providing a specialist resource to social services, health authorities, the prison and probation services, and police forces. All enquiries are treated in the strictest confidence.

Families Anonymous is a network of self-help groups focusing on the needs of the family and friends of drug abusers. About 60 groups currently meet in various parts of the UK.

Gambling

Gam-Anon, a sister organization of Gamblers Anonymous, provides a network of self-help groups for family and close friends of compulsive gamblers. It offers understanding and practical help for those suffering the fall-out from a gambler's damaging behaviour.

15

Prescription Drugs:
A special problem

So far the assumption behind our description of an 'addict' has been that he or she gradually, perhaps imperceptibly, becomes dependent on substances or behaviours they *know* to be mood altering. They do so, in short, for a buzz or a high and they do so wilfully and with the knowledge of the possible consequences. True, they may have chosen to ignore the consequences or perhaps believe they are strong enough to avoid them, but they know what they are getting into.

The tragedy is that once addiction and dependency have taken hold, the addict is trapped in a prison from which it is virtually impossible to escape by their efforts alone. At the outset, they drank, smoked cannabis, took cocaine or placed large sums of cash on the horses to feel better – even though there was no underlying physical condition they were trying to alleviate. It was a short-sighted and dangerous form of release or recreation.

However, with those addicted to benzodiazepines (which includes many prescription tranquillisers, sedatives and sleeping tablets) or dependent on the newer so-called SSRI (selective serotonin reuptake inhibitors) drugs (often prescription antidepressants), *this is not the case*. Here, men and women are prescribed a drug to relieve an underlying medical condition. Any suggestion of a recreational drug of choice is completely misplaced.

Many of these people unknowingly and unintentionally develop a habit that is every bit as damaging physically – and arguably more damaging psychologically – as a habit embarked on knowingly, because they often have no idea what is happening to them and why.

The 1960s and 1970s witnessed an explosion in the legal prescription of benzodiazepines for complaints as various as epilepsy, premenstrual tension and depression. Campaigners today argue that there was widespread ignorance at the time about the drug's side-effects and their highly addictive nature, and they were prescribed like sweets. The result was that after a comparatively short course, patients would report unwelcome reactions (effectively withdrawal symptoms) if they stopped taking them. They would return to the surgery for more and so the cycle would begin again. Any attempt to stop was so unpleasant and physically painful (some have said the withdrawal symptoms from certain prescription drugs are worse than heroin) that the only solution was to take more.

A decision to scale down the use of benzodiazepines was taken by successive UK governments but addiction charities say that the SSRI drugs that in part replaced them may be just as unpredictable in their side-effects. No official figures exist for SSRI dependency but it's estimated that some 1.5 million people are in some way dependent on benzodiazepines (campaigners say it could be up to twice that figure).

Many many men and women may have no idea why they are feeling as they are and may not even realize that they are clinically addicted.

If you have discovered you are among this group of people, the realization may come as a shock. You may feel that there is considerable stigma attached to being classed as a 'drug addict' when you've simply been following doctors' orders. The sense of shame and guilt you may feel is perfectly understandable – particularly if you belong to a generation when drug taking was less prevalent than it is today. Nonetheless, those feelings are completely misplaced. In most cases, your dependency will not be a result of weakness or self-indulgence but, more likely due to a faulty or misplaced diagnosis of a medical condition. Unfortunately, your own doctor may continue to prescribe you these drugs even when the medical condition has passed or is resistant to the increased dosage. If you are trying to reduce the dose unsuccessfully (because of the extreme discomfort), it's essential you raise this issue with your doctor. Perhaps do some research beforehand by calling one of the organizations listed at the end of this book or logging on to its website. Ask for independent guidance about how best to proceed.

Withdrawal symptoms can include:

- Restlessness

- Muscle and bone pain

- Night- and daytime cramps

- Insomnia

- Diarrhoea

- Vomiting

- Muscle spasms

- Cold flushes

- Depression or mood swings.

Under these circumstances of withdrawal, you may want to do anything to take away the pain – like getting a repeat prescription. Yet the prescription drugs may be doing you long-term harm so you have to end the course when your medical condition has improved. If you've become dependent you will need to be frank with your doctor and withdraw from the drug only under controlled medical supervision. What's happening, in effect, is a detoxification process that has to be professionally planned and monitored.

Based in Liverpool in the UK, the Council for Information on Tranquillisers and Antidepressants (CITA) is probably the nearest thing to a national helpline specifically for prescription drug addiction. It produces a wide range of literature on tranquillizers and antidepressants, drug reduction programmes, self-help and withdrawal problems.

It may be worth calling CITA to reassure yourself that you're not alone. You can be certain of a warm and friendly reception with no judgement or disapproval. Many of the volunteers will already know what you're going through, so you're are likely to feel immediately comfortable and reassured.

It is also worthwhile talking things over with a trusted friend or relative and asking them to accompany you to the surgery for moral support. Talk to your doctor firmly about your desire to reduce the dose and convince the doctor that you are serious about coming off antidepressants or tranquillizers. Ask for some no-nonsense information about your condition and ask him or her to give you some straight talking about what course of action is recommended.

You might need some moral support from your friend at a moment like this – especially if you're not the confrontational type. It's your health, body, and your long-term well-being that are at stake – you have a right for professionals to understand that. Even if it's out of character and at the risk of sounding too pushy, **make your feelings clear**.

A warning

Never buy drugs on the internet although it is increasingly easy to do so. The rise of so-called 'web pharmacies' has been blamed for an explosion in drug dependence throughout the UK. Buying drugs in this way – unseen, unsupervised and unchecked – is a possible sign that you have a problem with drug abuse and you are advised to seek immediate help.

Studies have shown that the relatively easy access to powerful painkillers, tranquillizers, benzodiazepines and antidepressants is leading to serious physical health problems. In a largely unregulated market, you have no way of knowing for sure whether the drugs are suitable for your own condition – or even whether they have been tampered with and could be doing you harm.

The rule is simple. Drugs should be prescribed by qualified doctors and dispensed by qualified pharmacists.

16

Other resources

We hope this book has provided you with a basic toolkit for your own long-term personal maintenance. Here are some more resources that may come in handy in your new and improved life.

Mental growth

You now have a future with limitless possibilities undulled by chemicals and destructive patterns of behaviour. We want to encourage you to make the most of it. You've done nothing less than change your life – with enormous personal and shared effort. Having achieved so much, there may be other challenges you can rise to. You may be able to take your life into a dimension that you could never have dreamed of. The phrase 'What does not kill you makes you stronger' comes to mind. Perhaps there is other strength and energy that you can tap into.

We're not talking about a magical transformation into Superman or Superwoman, but the possibility of real growth. You might want to develop your mind, for instance, in a way you couldn't have done when you were addicted. Consider enrolling on a full- or part-time course as a mature student, studying to gain qualifications that will enable you to make a career change in mid-life. Get involved in local politics or in local community or environmental issues. You may simply want to read more and learn new things simply for their own sake. Or you might have an idea for a small business which, with the application you once lacked, you could turn into a real going concern. With a clear head and a realistic assessment of you talents, aspirations, and your finances, you can now begin to think of life changing projects.

You don't have to have such grand designs to grow mentally, of course. There are a million and one other smaller ways in which you can grow. Take on an allotment, for example, and borrow a few books from the library about planting your own vegetables – this can be as intellectually satisfying as learning about mathematics or ancient history. Do what suits your temperament. There are opportunities there for the taking.

In Part 1, you may remember, at the point you first sought help, we advised you against making big decisions. You were in no fit state to emigrate to the other side of the world, move house or have a baby. Things may be different now. You may be ready to make a major change. Only you can decide. Weigh up the circumstances and take a measured view. You may be at a second crossroads in your life. Whereas before some roads led to destruction and some to salvation, this time all roads lead to the promise of a new life.

Emotional growth

You've certainly had your emotional ups and downs over the past few months or maybe years. It's a pretty fair bet to say you've learned a lot about your inner life – that life of emotions and feelings that for so many of us remains a closed book. Now you've examined it and seen how important it is, you may want to develop that side of yourself more.

At the very least, your experiences may help you to understand better how people tick. You may find yourself more sympathetic to other people now you can see the pressures that have made them act in the way they do. Where you may once have seen the world in black and white, perhaps you're beginning to realize it's made up of quite a lot of different shades of grey.

Now that you're free of the old addictions and have been forced to learn some painful emotional truths about yourself, you can start to learn some surprising truths about other people. Growing in understanding and in compassion could be one of the most important (and possibly unlikely) outcomes you could have imagined from this episode in your life.

This period in your life is an experience that's taught you a lot. Hang on to it. This doesn't mean living in the past; it means learning from your past so that you can go on to live a more productive life in the future. We have talked about your new life in terms of a career change or simply a new attitude of mind; emotional growth is something far more subtle – more like a change of heart.

You might want to find out more about the workings of the human personality. You'll almost certainly find that any novel you read now will be read in a completely different state of mind. Having explored your own emotions quite thoroughly, you'll be better equipped to understand the emotions that drive other people – whether in real life or in fiction. You might even want to explore your own emotions more deeply with a trained therapist who, with your cooperation, can teach you even more about yourself.

Of course, this isn't for everyone, and realistically most people will be content to go on living broadly the same life as before but with a greater appreciation of it. There's a heroism in doing the ordinary things in life well and with a full appreciation of what life has to offer in all its fullness – rather than taking the chemical short cuts to temporary pleasure that turn out to be no pleasure at all. At its very simplest, if you can go for a picnic with family and friends and enjoy it even when the weather turns stormy and you're forced to eat soggy sandwiches in a car with the windows steamed up, or if you can get pleasure walking along a road or sitting on a park bench talking to a mate, you're doing something very important. You're starting to develop an inner emotional life that can thrive by itself without the constant illusory stimulations of alcohol, drugs or gambling.

Spiritual growth

Finally, we come to that area that those familiar with the 12-step Alcoholics Anonymous programme will recognize. This is a controversial area and one that some of you may be inclined to reject straightaway. By 'spiritual growth' we don't mean religious belief. We mean that important something in life that we can't quite put our finger on, something that often seems outside ourselves.

You may be shifting uneasily in your seat at this point. You might say there is nothing outside ourselves, there is only what we can comprehend with our mind and our senses and any talk of the spirit is nonsense. We respect that view, and perhaps this final section is not for you, so simply skip over it.

However, by 'spiritual growth' we mean a kind of calm acceptance of the way life is and a resignation – without bitterness or complaint – at what life has to offer. That doesn't mean we hold our hands up and let life happen to us. We have to do our bit to change and influence it (and that will mean there are times when we have to struggle and to fight). But it does mean growing in understanding and, having changed what we can, accepting what we can't – again without bitterness or complaint.

Spiritual growth, as we see it, is growing in wisdom and maturity, accepting that there are mysteries in life that will not be explained. It means facing up to sickness and loss, contemplating the loss of a loved one with sadness but also with the hope that life will go on, rather than reaching for the bottle because you feel you can't go on. Ultimately, spiritual growth means contemplating the inevitability of our own departure from this earth with resignation and peace of mind. However, between the moment you finish this sentence and the moment (let it be a long way off) you draw your final breath, there is something rather important. It's called life. A life free of the old addictions. Enjoy it to the full.

Part 6:
More Help
at Hand

Alcohol

Al-Anon Family Groups
61 Great Dover Street
London SE1 4YF
Helpline: 020 7403 0888
www.al-anonuk.org.uk

Alcohol Concern
First floor
8 Shelton Street
London WC2H 9JR
Tel: 020 7395 4000
www.alcoholconcern.org.uk

Alcohol Education and Research Council
Room 178, Queen Anne Business Centre
28 Broadway
London SW1H 9JX
Tel: 020 7340 9502
www.aerc.org.uk

Alcohol Services for the Community
26–30 John Street
Luton
Beds, LU1 2JE
Tel: 01582 723434
www.alcohol-services.co.uk

Alcoholics Anonymous
General Service Office
PO Box 1
10 Toft Green
York YO1 7ND
National Helpline: 0845 769 7555
(calls charged at local rate)
www.alcoholics-anonymous.org.uk

National Association for the Children of Alcoholics (NACOA)
PO Box 64
Fishponds
Bristol BS16 2UH
Helpline: 0800 358 3456
www.nacoa.org.uk

Publications by NACOA

Information for Children of Alcoholics
*Some Mums and Dads Drink Too Much and Use
    Drugs*
*A Guide for Schools: Children of Alcoholics in the
    Classroom*

Drug and substance abuse

Addaction
67–69 Cowcross Street
London EC1M 6PU
Tel: 020 7251 5860 (office hours)
www.addaction.org.uk

Adfam
25 Corsham Street
London N1 6DR
Tel: 020 7553 7642
www.adfam.org.uk

DrugScope
40 Bermondsey Street,
London SE1 3UD
Tel: 020 7940 7500
www.drugscope.org.uk

Families Anonymous
The Doddington and Rollo Community
Association
Charlotte Despard Avenue
London SW11 5HD
Helpline: 0845 1200 660
www.famanon.org.uk

National Drugs Helpline (Talk to Frank)
Tel: 0800 77 66 00 (24 hours)
www.talktofrank.com

Narcotics Anonymous
UK Service Office
202 City Road
London EC1V 2PH
Tel: 0845 3733366 or 020 7730 0009
www.ukna.org

Publications by Narcotics Anonymous

Journeys
A series of seven booklets exploring the needs of different family members in different situations. They provide both real life stories and practical advice.
Guides for Families
Prison Series
Tough Love
The Twelve Steps of Families Anonymous
Guide for the Family of the Drug Abuser
Twelve Steps Workbook
Does Someone You Care About Use Drugs?

Prescription drugs

Benzo.org.uk
A private web-based benzodiazepine withdrawal forum and advice line. Membership by application and approval.

Bristol and District Tranquilliser Project
88 Henleaze Road
Henleaze
Bristol BS99 1XP
Helpline: 0117 962 8874 (Mon–Thurs
10 a.m.–4 p.m.)

Codeinefree.org.uk
A web-based self-help group providing advice, information, and support by people who know from personal experience the effects and implications of Codeine addiction.

Council for Information on Tranquillisers and Antidepressants (CITA)
JDI Centre,
3–11 Mersey View
Waterloo
Liverpool L22 6QA
Helpline: 0151 932 0102 (10 a.m.–1 p.m. daily)

www.citawithdrawal.org.uk
www.backtolife.uk.com

Publications by CITA

Back to Life
A book describing tranquillizer addiction and withdrawal.
Alive and Kicking
One man's battle against tranquillizers

Gambling

Gam-Anon
PO Box 5382
London W1A 6SA
Helpline: 08700 50 88 80 (24 hours)
www.gamanon.org.uk

Gamblers Anonymous
PO Box 5382
London W1A 6SA
Tel: 0207 384 3040
www.gamblersanonymous.org.uk

CONCLUSION

Thank you for taking the time and effort to get this far. It may be too much to read the book in one go, but you can dip into it whenever you need to. Ignore what's not appropriate to your own life and add the things that are. This is a guide book, not an instruction manual.

How can we sum up what we've learned together in the course of the preceding pages? If we had to boil it down to three key words, they would be:

- Control

- Community

- Compassion.

Control

By control we mean self-control but also more than that. It means controlling appetites, cravings, temptations and so on, but also having control over the course and direction of your life. For too long, you have allowed bad habits to control you. You had no power over them at all and the bottle, the pills or the gambling ruled your life.

At great personal cost, you decided that things were not going to control you anymore; you were going to control them. You broke the chains of your addiction and took control over your own life. The challenge is to keep control and not let it slip.

With this control, probably for the first time in a long time, came personal responsibility, the idea that you had a duty to yourself as an adult to act in an adult way. Getting drunk every night, crashing out on the sofa, slumping semi-conscious in a chair anaesthetized by drugs, or biting your nails over the throw of the dice was essentially childishly dependent behaviour. With commendably strong resolve, you took on the full responsibility of being an adult. A surprisingly difficult thing to do and one that many people never master!

Having taken responsibility for yourself, you have begun to understand what it means to take responsibility for others. In the first instance, this means responsibility to partners and children – to those who look to you to provide comfort, companionship and support (none of which an addict can provide). Second, it means taking responsibility to keep friendships alive. Relationships are like fires. They need fuel or they go out. Make the effort to keep in touch, phone, write or email, just to chat and to ask how the other person is, rather than waiting until you need a favour from them. This responsibility leads to the second principle in your new life – community.

Community

Community is feeling part of the world beyond yourself and your family. It means taking part in the interdependent life that we all share. Locked in the isolation of addiction, there was no way you could take part in anything. Indeed, in your own tiny world there was nothing to take part in and, worse, no one to share that nothingness with. There can be no worse torment than being so completely alone. Welcome back to the world of real community.

Compassion

The third key to a fulfilling new life is compassion, which in a sense flows from control and community. What you have been through may give you some understanding and tolerance of others. You might be able to be slower to judge and quicker to listen to your fellow human being, if you weren't before.

Your compassion will extend to any recovering addict you might meet – you may even be sponsoring and mentoring one already. Moreover, the understanding you've acquired in very testing circumstances will help you to extend that compassion to more than your immediate circle. In this way, you can look at your illness and recovery as a positive experience from which you have learned and grown. It hasn't destroyed you, so we can only conclude that it's made you stronger. Well done.

Finally, our shared journey is at an end. To recovering addicts and carers alike, thank you for allowing us to accompany you. We wish you well for a future that will contain many new people and many new experiences. Enjoy them to the full.

Also available from *This Morning* and Hodder Education are:

- This Morning: Get Out of Debt

- This Morning: Beat Your Depression

- This Morning: Overcome Your Postnatal Depression

- This Morning: Cope With Infertility

- This Morning: Escape Domestic Violence

- This Morning: Cope With Bereavement

- This Morning: Get Over Your Break-up